13 KEYS TO GENIUS

Ryan Palmer

Copyright © 2013 by Ryan O. P. Palmer
All rights reserved. This book or any portion thereof may not be reproduced or used in any manner whatsoever without the express written permission of the publisher except for the use of brief quotations in a book review.

Printed in the United States of America
First Printing, 2013

ISBN-13: 978-1492812326
ISBN-10: 1492812323
BISAC: Education / Educational Psychology

Contact the author at roppalmer@hotmail.com

13 Keys To Genius

To Mommy and Daddy

Ryan Palmer

13 Keys To Genius

Table of Contents

Preface v
    The DNA of Excellent Learning and Learners vi
    Learning as an active state ix
    The 13 Keys to Genius xii
    Psychological, Emotional, and Social Laws...................xii
    ACKNOWLEDGMENTS xv

Chapter 1: Law of Self-Belief—If we are to achieve, we must first self-believe..1
    Self-Efficacy and Achievement 2
    How can we strengthen our sense of self-efficacy? 6
    References 12

Chapter 2: The Law of Responsibility—The outcomes of our lives come out of our life's decisions...........................14
    Locus of Control and Academic Performance..............15
    How can we become internal in our locus of control?.19

Law 3: To achieve academic success you must be motivated by academic success. 25
    Motivation Makes Us Limitless....................................25
    Achievement Motivation and Academic Performance.28
    From the Prosaic to the Poetic 30
    Arousing and Maintaining Motivation........................32

Law 4: Be anxious about nothing if you want to achieve something 38
    Manage Stress To Do your Best On High-Stakes Tests .38
    Good Stress vs. Bad Stress 41

    The Brain and Distress 42

    Testing For Success 44

    Learning to Relax 45

Law 5: The Law of Goal-Setting—To achieve big, we must dream big 50

    The Race to the Moon 50

    Goal-Setting and Academic Performance 52

    Being Smart About Goal-Setting 57

    References 61

Law 6: The Law of Engagement—There can be no great achievement without great commitment 66

    Changing the world in 9.58 seconds 66

    Student Engagement 68

    Mind Where You Sit 70

    Promoting Engagement 73

Law 7: Self-discipline opens the door to academic achievement 76

    Your life in a Marshmallow 76

    Self-discipline and Academic Achievement 79

    Developing Self-Control 80

CHAPTER 8: The law of collaboration—learning occurs in community 90

    Social contagion 90

    No Man Is An Island 92

    Collaboration and achievement 93

    Why it works 94

    Benefits 96

    Collaborating for best results: Recommendations 101

References 104

Chapter 9: Law of Rest—If we are to be academically deep, we must sleep! 106

    Sleeping is for Wimps? 106

    Academic Performance and Sleep Quality/Quantity ..108

    Snooze and Lose [9] 110

    Sleep Quality 111

Chapter 10: Live right to learn right—Healthy choices and Mindfulness 117

    Academic Performance and Healthy Living: The Research 120

    Alcohol, Tobacco, and Drug Use 120

    Diet and Exercise 122

    The mechanics 125

    Recommendation 127

    Summary of Dietary Guidelines 130

    Chapter 11: The Law of Exercise 136

    Challenging the Times 136

    Sound body for a sound mind 138

    Exercise and academic achievement 140

    Exercises: How they work and which one works for you 144

    Exercise and you 147

    Recommendations and Actionable Strategies 149

Chapter 12: The Law of readiness 155

    The Laws of Learning 155

    Readiness to learn 157

    Getting prepared 159

Time Management 160
Skills for Learning: During the Class 165
Revision: Learning and Relearning 170
Deliberate Practice 171
APPENDIX 174
The Cornell System ....
Chapter 13: The Law of study and deliberate practice 178
Exploring self-regulated learning 178
The DNA of the self-regulated learner 179
Help seeking, Peer Learning, and Social Control 184
Organizing and Transforming Information 186
Rehearsing and Memorizing 187
Environment management 188
External factors affecting self-regulated learning 191
Self-regulated learning strategies 192
Study and Learning Strategies [18] 196
Biography of the Author 204

Preface

Learning is a powerful dynamic for personal transformation and self-actualization. Learning, I claim, is the only way for an individual to become renewed—to become transformed. The apostle Paul, writing to the Roman church, puts it this way: Do not be conformed to this world but be transformed, by the renewing of your mind…" As Charlie "Tremendous" Jones has affirmed, in five years' time, two things will change us: the books we have read and the people we have met (Giambalvo, n.d.).

Learning is that catalyst, in the Newtonian economy of the word, that accelerates or decelerates this journey to change and personal transformation. This book aspires to be catalytic, to power its readers into a lifestyle that makes learning—and the desire to learn—second nature, by unearthing the emotional, social, and physical drivers of a state of being that is ready to learn, and therefore which finds learning satisfying, and not frustrating.

The DNA of Excellent Learning and Learners

What are the characteristics of those who learn well? How do we learn? How can we become effective learners? There is a fundamental and unquestioned assumption that we make when we go into any classroom or learning situation: that we know *how to* learn. There are three primary tenets to skill in learning: aptitude; attitude; and, application. This book urges that we can learn those skills, practise them, and grow in our effective use of them so that they come to our aid in achieving superior academic outcomes.

Learning is a multi-dimensional and multi-sensory process. We use all of our senses—feeling, smelling, tasting, hearing, and seeing—in the learning process. Learning is, therefore, intensely physiological, social, and emotional. Deep learning is best promoted when we integrate mind, body, and emotions—that is, when thinking, doing, and feeling are fused in cognitive agreement. If we take a systems-approach to learning, we understand that student performance hinges on multiple variables. Huitt et al. (2009) argue that student achievement is a multi-variable process impacted upon by home, school, classroom, and student characteristics.

This book focusses on student characteristics and student behavior, because these are the variables that a student has immediate control and influence over. It is consonant with the attitudes and approaches of Benjamin Franklin, a renowned polymath—a person of extensive learning and who commands knowledge in a range of fields of study. A founding father of the United States of America, Benjamin Franklin, in brief, was a political theorist, politician, statesman, diplomat, civic activist, scientist, musician, inventor, printer, and author.

Barry Zimmerman, noted educational psychologist and a leader in thinking about effective student learning behavior, introduces the model of successful learning that this book returns to frequently. Zimmerman (1990) reflects on the example of Franklin and identifies the traditions and characteristics of independent or "self-regulated" learning. He stated:

Since the founding of the republic, American educational leaders have stressed the importance of individuals assuming personal responsibility and control for their own acquisition of knowledge and skill. Benjamin Franklin wrote extensively in his autobiography about techniques he used to improve his learning, erudition, and self-control (*Benjamin Franklin Writings,* 1868/1987). He described in detail how he set learning goals for himself, recording his daily progress in a ledger. He sought to improve his writing by selecting exemplary written models and attempting to emulate the authors' prose. In addition to teaching himself to write, Franklin felt this procedure improved his memory and his "arrangement of thoughts," two cognitive benefits that research on observational learning has verified (Rosenthal & Zimmerman, 1978; Zimmerman & Rosenthal, 1974). Recognition of the importance of personal initiative in learning has been reaffirmed by contemporary national leaders such as Gardner (1963), former Secretary of Health, Education, and Welfare, who suggested that "the ultimate goal of the education system is to shift to the individual the burden of pursuing his own education."

Learning as an active state

This book challenges the reader to engage in this type of active rather than passive learning: to not simply become a receptacle for information transmitted by authoritative others, but to engage in the process of constructing one's own knowledge through questioning, updating, and integrating the old and the new. As Martin Fischer, physician and author, advises, "The pupil only can educate himself. Teachers are the custodians of apparatus upon which he himself must turn and twist to acquire the excellences that distinguish the better from the poorer of God's vessels."

Learning is about connecting: connecting with prior learning, connecting with the material, connecting to other learners, and connecting to the real world. As Marvin Minsky, cognitive scientist and philosopher states it, "You don't understand anything until you learn it more than one way." It is when we make multiple connections, learn something in multiple ways, that we can secure our memories, and improve our ability to retrieve same information.

When most people write about the laws of learning, what they really mean are the laws of *teaching and learning.* In other words, how can a teacher better cooperate with the learner to mutually secure the learning outcomes. This book, however, looks at how the learner, independent of the actions of the school or teacher, can improve his or her chances of understanding the content taught, and of being successful in a formal educational setting.

It also offers students practical understanding and tools to grow in the application of the principles of active and effective learning. In doing so, it seeks to dispel some of the myths often bandied about and which have introduced confusion in the conversation about how we learn. Based on the research of cognitive scientists (Carey, 2010) it affirms that regular testing is good, that studying in different places is to be preferred than one place, that mixed reviews is preferred to just practising one topic/idea, and that pacing one's studying is superior to cramming.

After an extensive review of the academic performance literature I have found convergence on what I call the 13 Keys of Genius, or "Laws" that govern the attainment of superior learning outcomes. These factors have been placed into two broad categories: 1) the psychological, emotional, and social aspects of learning; and 2) the behavioral and physical factors of successful learning.

The 13 Keys to Genius

Psychological, Emotional, and Social Laws

1. **Self-Belief:** You must believe in order to achieve.

2. **Responsibility**: If it is to be, it has to be me.

3. **Motivation**: To arrive, you must have the drive.

4. **Relaxation**: Manage stress to do your best on high-stakes tests.

5. **Goal-Setting**: To achieve big, we must dream big.

6. **Engagement**: There can be no great achievement without great commitment.

7. **Self-Discipline**: If you want to roll, you must have self-control.

8. **Collaboration**: To correct, we must connect.

Personal Management Laws

9. **Rest**: To do our best our body must have adequate rest.

10. **Exercise**: If you exercise true, it will be the best thing you do.

11. **Healthy Choices**: If you straighten up and live right, you will be academically bright.

12. **Readiness**: To learn you need to be ready, and then

learning will be steady.

13. **Study**: Great achievement requires great effort.

References

Carey, B. (2010, September 6). Forget What You Know About Good Study Habits. The New York Times. Retrieved from http://www.nytimes.com/

Giambalvo, S. About Being Tremendous. Retrieved from http://www.modeweekly.com/1996/0896/0896CharlieJones.htm

Huitt, W., Huitt, M., Monetti, D., & Hummel, J. (2009). A systems-based synthesis of research related to improving students' academic performance. Paper presented at the 3rd International City Break Conference sponsored by the Athens Institute for Education and Research (ATINER), October 16-19, Athens, Greece. Retrieved 2012/12/03 from http://www.edpsycinteractive.org/papers/improving-school-achievement.pdf

Zimmerman, B. J. (1990). Self-regulated learning and academic achievement: An overview. Educational Psychologist, 25 (1), 3-17. Doi:10.1207/s15326985ep2501_2

ACKNOWLEDGMENTS

Sincere appreciation to John Bello and Maria Palmer Bello for the ideational and financial support in driving this project through to fruition. Thanks must also be extended to Nikishia Greenidge and Nickesha Senior for providing seminal chapter materials to assisting in the unpacking the thesis of the book. Many thanks to Wordsharp.net who provided editorial services and facilitated the preparation of the material for e-publication. Final thanks to Margaret Clarke for efforts expended in an initial cover design for the book.

Ryan Palmer

CHAPTER 1: LAW OF SELF-BELIEF—IF WE ARE TO ACHIEVE, WE MUST FIRST SELF-BELIEVE

We can only build ... with faith in ourselves and with self-reliance, believing in our own possibilities.
—Marcus Mosiah Garvey, Jr.

Born into a large family of six in 1927, Cesar Chavez and his family faced the economic reversals and injustices that attended the Great Depression, as well as confronted the prejudices against Mexican-Americans at school and in the army. From working on the farms to organizing farm workers, Chavez, armed with only an eight-grade education, fought to improve wages and to gain collective bargaining rights for farm workers. The principal tools he employed were fasts, strikes, and boycotts.

Throughout the 1960s and 1970s, these strategies, orchestrated through the United Farm Workers (UFW), were instrumental in achieving higher wages and bargaining agreements for farm workers. At the heart of this movement and other similar civil rights organizations, and fuelling Chavez's passionate energies and actions, was the simple refrain: Sí, se puede—a cry that would be adopted by a young black senator from Chicago, in his own political campaign: Yes, we can! [1]

Chavez became a transformational leader because he had a transformational belief. "Yes it can be done" became an article of faith, and an unyielding foundation of hopeful and inspired action that affected how he faced down the adversities present in his environment. Despite the contradictions of his adolescent upbringing—poverty, injustice and prejudice—he was resilient and unwavering in his belief that what he desired, he could achieve.

Self-Efficacy and Achievement

This is the principal and primary law, and on this law rests all other laws of learning: we must first believe that we are able to accomplish any task we set out to accomplish. We must be confident about our ability to learn! Psychologists call this belief in our ability to succeed our self-efficacy. Albert Bandura (1986), regarded as one of the greatest living psychologists, and founder of social learning theory and the theory of self-efficacy, urges that "among the different aspects of self-knowledge, perhaps none is more influential in people's everyday lives than conceptions of their personal efficacy." The belief in one's ability to succeed, and that one can grow in that ability—rather than see ability as permanently fixed or low—are critical ingredients in performance and achievement. This is a truth that religions have long understood: that to see, we must first believe.

Marcus Garvey Jr., the first black man to successfully organize blacks on a large scale, and boasting a membership of two to four million in his pan-African organization (Universal Negro Improvement Association, UNIA) recognized the vitality of self-confidence. He asserted that, "If you have no confidence in self, you are twice defeated in the race of life. With confidence, you win even before you have started."

Garvey understood that no sphere of human activity could see success if it did not begin with positive self-belief. However, he also appreciated that self-belief must be coupled with self-reliance, resilience, and effort. He expounded this as follows (Garvey, 1986):

So few of us can understand what it takes to make a man—the man who will never say die; the man who will never give up; the man who will never depend on others to do for him what he ought to do for himself; the man who will not blame God; who will not blame Nature, who will not blame Fate for his condition; but the man who will go out and make conditions to suit himself.

Research indicates that academic learning and achievement, and intrinsic motivation are strongly influenced by having a high sense of self-efficacy. Indeed, confidence aids in improving student performance (Pressley et al., 1987). Students with high self-efficacy approach rather than avoid challenging tasks, and maintain mental fortitude even when faced with contradictions, setbacks, and disappointments in their personal circumstances. Self-efficacy has been found to be the best indicator of student success as it provides the basis for intrinsic motivation, supports the achievement of academic excellence, and helps the individual to overcome in the face of life's adversities (Coutinho & Neuman, 2008; Pearson, 2008; Surland, 2010).

Students who exhibit low self-efficacy follow a self-fulfilling prophecy by believing that they cannot or will not be successful. Their effort level endures only for a short time, and they avoid any task perceived to be difficult. With such low aspirations and low effort, low achievement easily follows (Margolis and McCabe, 2006; Bandura, 1994). As Alexandre Dumas rendered it, "A man who doubts himself is like a man who would enlist in the ranks of his enemies and bear arms against himself. He makes his failures certain by himself being the first person to be convinced of it."

What do we now understand? Students who expect to succeed will work harder than those who do not (Latu, 2004). Additionally, this expectation of future success is important if motivation is to be maintained (Dornyei, 2001)

How can we strengthen our sense of self-efficacy?

Several strategies are available to us to improve our sense of self-efficacy. First, we must recognize that our beliefs affect our thoughts, our thoughts influence our feelings, and our feelings affect our actions: these father the outcomes in our lives. If we are not happy with the outcomes, we must go to their root, and change the nature and direction of our beliefs. We must relinquish any deficit thinking that says we cannot achieve or do not have the ability to succeed, and refresh our mindset with positive affirmations that agree with the results that we would like to see. T. Harv Eker (2005), author of the *Secrets of the Millionaire Mind*, frames it as follows, "In order to change your results you need to unlearn the old ways of thinking that were causing you to fail." Thinking positively means that when setbacks occur we should replace the old thoughts of, 'I am just unlucky' or 'I knew I couldn't do it,' with 'I didn't study comprehensively enough' or 'I didn't spend enough time in preparation.' The latter phrases affirm that by studying more or spending more time, we are able to achieve the results we desire.

Second, we can refresh our mindset by setting moderate goals that allow us opportunities to succeed. Students who set their own goals have a higher level of motivation to achieve them, than if someone else set the goals for them (Hom & Murphy, 1983). As an anonymous contributor has noted, "Self-confidence is the memory of success." Keeping a portfolio of our successes can feed our self-confidence and help to grow a new mental attitude of possibility.

Third, we must be able to visualize our success, or as Stephen Covey (1997) puts it in *7 Habits of Highly Effective People*, we must see the end from the beginning. This ability is the outgrowth of possibility thinking, and can be strengthened by observing peers and successful others who have overcome similar challenges. Seeing others succeed where we have failed can help to give us the motivation we need, as well as guide us in how to plan for success.

Fourth, adopt strategies that will enable you to succeed. This has multiple layers. It means using failure as feedback, that is, learning from your mistakes and understanding what went wrong and why. Next, build momentum by putting in the work early—putting in the extra discipline to score well on homework and quizzes can set the right tone for the semester. Cement your momentum by building effective study/research networks. Having a consistent study group through your college career can help promote smooth and accelerated learning. Additionally, build positive relationships with professors as they can help to clarify the material or to direct you to where additional help can be gathered.

Fifth, build routines that will promote your success. Primarily, this involves brutally scrutinizing how you use your most valuable resource—your time. Thinking through what our goals are, and outlining a plan to achieve those goals help to buffer or block failure. Failing to commit our time means that others can borrow our time to the expense of achieving our priority goals. Planning and building routines therefore enable us to say no to *good ideas*, which are the enemies of the *best ideas.* Planning our time fixes a time-budget to get the hard work done. Planning our time should also include opportunities for reflection: to identify and improve on approaches to studying and learning; and, on how we can build more effctive learning partnerships.

Sixth, know when it is appropriate to quit. Sometimes it is possible to win a battle but lose the war. In choosing our wars, the first thing we must be assured of is the possibility of victory. If our planning fails to properly evaluate our ability to succeed in a course, regardless of efforts to use our time more productively and seek help, then it may be that the course, or major, is not for us. Being brave enough to walk away can save us the futility and frustration of further unrewarded efforts—and will open up new opportunities for directing our creative and intellectual energies.

Finally, associate with others who will affirm your possibility. Successful others not only model the strategies and possibilities of success, but they can be a source of positive encouragement. Develop a network of friends and family members who will encourage and support you as you move toward your goals. This also requires you to resolve any personal or emotional issues in friendships or family that may be consuming your heart time and mind time. Forgiving and letting go can be an important step in freeing your creative energies—opening up your heart and mind to your own goals.

13 Keys To Genius

Famous Quotes about Self-Efficacy	Personalities
Self-confidence is the first requisite to great undertakings.	Samuel Johnson
Nothing can be done without hope and confidence	Helen Keller
They are able who think they are able	Virgil
Whether you think that you can or you can't, you're usually right	Henry Ford
Skill and confidence are an unconquered army	George Herbert
If I have the belief that I can do it, I shall surely acquire the capacity to do it even if I may not have it at the beginning.	Mahatma Gandhi
It is our duty as human beings to proceed as though the limits of our capabilities do not exist.	Teilhard de Chardin

References

Bandura, Albert (1986). Social Foundations of Thought and Action: A social cognitive theory. Englewood Cliffs, N.J.: Prentice Hall.

Bandura, A. (1994). Self-efficacy. In V. S. Ramachaudran (Ed.), *Encyclopedia of human behavior* (Vol. 4, pp. 71-81). New York: Academic Press. (Reprinted in H. Friedman (Ed.), Encyclopedia of mental health. San Diego: Academic Press, 1998).

Coutinho, S. A. and Neuman, G. (2008). A model of metacognition, achievement goal orientation, learning style and self-efficacy. *Learning Environment Res.* 11, p. 131-151.

Covey, S. R. (1997). *The 7 habits of highly effective families.* St. Martin's Press.

Dörnyei, Z. (2001). *Teaching and researching motivation.* Allyn & Bacon.

Eker, T. H. (2005). Secrets of the millionaire mind: Mastering the inner game of wealth. Harper Business.

Garvey, M (1986). *Philosophy and Opinions of Marcus Garvey or Africa for the Africans.* A. J. Garvey (Ed.). Massachusetts, MA: First Majority Press.

Hom, H. L., Jr., & Murphy, M.D. (1983). Low achiever's performance: The positive impact of a self- directed goal. *Personality and Social Psychology Bulletin*, 11, 275-285.

Latu, V. F. (2004). There is more to learning mathematics than mathematics: Attributional beliefs and motivation of Maori and Pacific Island students. In Mathematics education for the third millennium: Towards 2010: Proceedings of the 27th annual conference of the

Mathematics Education Research Group of Australasia, Townsville, 27th-30th June (Vol. 2, pp. 343-350).

Margolis, H., McCabe, P. (2006, March). *Intervention in School and Clinic, 41*(4), p 218-227.

McGuire, M (2010). Three Simple Words: A Rhetorical Analysis of the Slogan "Yes WE Can". *Advances in Communication Theory and Research.* Vol 3. Retrieved from http://www.k-state.edu/actr/category/2010/default.htm

Pajares, F. (n.d). *Information on Self-Efficacy.* Retrieved December 5, 2012, from http://www.uky.edu/~eushe2/Pajares/self-efficacy.html

Pearson, M.M. (2008). Voices of hope. *Education and Urban Society, 41*(1), 80-103.

Pressley, M., Borkowski, J. G., & Schneider, W. (1987). Cognitive strategies: Good strategy users coordinate metacognition and knowledge. In R. Vasta & G. Whitehurst (Eds.), *Annals of child development* (Vol. 5, pp. 89-129). Greenwich, CT: JAI Press.

Surland, R. (2010). *Student Voices: Self-Efficacy and Graduating High School.* (Doctoral dissertation). Retrieved from http://soar.wichita.edu/xmlui/bitstream/handle/10057/3290/d10012_Surland.pdf?sequence=1

CHAPTER 2: THE LAW OF RESPONSIBILITY—THE OUTCOMES OF OUR LIVES COME OUT OF OUR LIFE'S DECISIONS

If you haven't the strength to impose your own terms upon life, you must accept the terms it offers.
—T. S. Eliot

A chief is a man who assumes responsibility. He says, "I was beaten," he does not say "My men were beaten."
—Antoine de Saint-Exupery

Light and Invention

How does one make an incandescent light bulb that is bright and safe enough for home use, that has a long life, and that can be produced economically? This was a set of problems that arrested inventors at the dawn of the nineteenth century. Before Joseph Swan and Thomas Edison, there were some twenty-two inventors over a span of seventy-five years who came close with a variety of solutions, but who were still unable to solve the quadruple problem of safety, visibility, durability, and economy.

When Edison attempted to solve this problem, it took him some two years, more than a thousand failed attempts, and over six thousand different fibers to light his bulb and the world. Edison, reflecting upon his approach, declared, "If I find ten thousand ways something won't work, I haven't failed. I am not discouraged, because every wrong attempt discarded is another step forward."

Edison, regarded as one of the greatest inventors of all times, demonstrates for us a way of seeing failure as feedback: providing information that the methods employed were incorrect, or that the application level was inadequate for the given task. He did not say to himself, "I am so stupid. I am a failure. I give up!" On the contrary, he refused to see failure as a personal flaw. He refused to doubt himself.

Locus of Control and Academic Performance

When you fail or succeed on a test, do you say to yourself that you studied hard for the test, that you spent enough time preparing for the test, and that the result was therefore expected? Alternatively, do you say that it was luck, or that the teacher was feeling kind or mean on that particular day?

Students, who ascribe their success or failure to their own effort, or lack thereof, are described as having an internal locus of control. Others, who see their performance as contingent on the teacher, luck, or other environmental factors are described as having an external locus of control. Extensive research confirms the common sense understanding that individuals with a strong orientation of responsibility, and who are confident about their abilities, perform better academically. Research also evidences that students who have an internal locus of control not only achieve higher grades, but also tend to procrastinate less, and exhibit lower levels of test anxiety relative to those students with external locus of control (Gifford et al., 2006; Carden et al., 2004).

Students with an internal locus of control tend to have successful study strategies, and manage stress and time constraints better. They demonstrate greater ownership and responsibility for their learning (Wolk & Bloom, 1978; Findley & Cooper, 1983; Grimes, Millea & Woodruff, 2004). These students tend to be resilient and to vary the things in their control in order to change an unsatisfactory outcome to a desired one. Students with an external locus of control tend to have poor study habits, do not manage stress well, earn lower grades, and blame others for their underperformance. The process of blaming others, their environment, Fate or God allows them to protect their self-esteem in the face of low achievement (Basgall & Snyder, 1988; Luther, 1991).

Suh and Suh (2006) studied 1,430 students who did not graduate from high school and who continued forward to earn a first degree. They found that personal management skills, academic goal setting, and internal locus of control were the primary determinants of degree attainment.

Having an internal locus of control means that we can trust or rely on ourselves to generally come through on a task we set before us. It tells us that the individual will persevere, apply extended effort, resourcefully problem-solve, and adapt from previous experiences to accomplish the desired goal (King, 2006). Those who do not have this internal locus of control are more likely to believe that they cannot control the factors that contribute to goal attainment, develop a sense of helplessness or dependency, tend not to believe in the possibility of improvement, and carry an expectation that they will fail (Anderman & Midgley, 1997; Seifert, 2004).

The take away truth from the above discussion is that what we believe matters. Our beliefs contain a psychological force that affects our expectations of future success, and that helps to determine our behavioral responses (Weiner, 1985). If we believe that the teacher should explain everything, that learning is about rote memorization of definitions, procedures and formulas, then this can conflict with truly mastering the subject and diminish student effort (Latu, 2004). If we believe "if it is to be, it is up to me," then we will be empowered to grasp responsibility for achieving our learning outcomes, to apply effort and time, and to creatively problem-solve.

How can we become internal in our locus of control?

As Jim Rohn, motivational speaker and author, asserts, "Your life does not get better by chance, it gets better by change." This tells us that we should understand that we have a choice, and not deciding is itself a choice. We can choose our life outcomes or let others and our circumstances choose for us. To move from an external locus of control to an internal one, externals must therefore change the way they talk to themselves, and how they attribute causes to outcomes. This may involve making positive affirmations aloud, in a whisper, silently, as well as writing these affirmations down in conspicuous places where they will be seen daily. Such affirmations may involve saying:

- I can do this.
- I won't quit.
- Excellence is my signature.
- Achievers sacrifice for success.
- I must study harder to go higher.

In developing a more hopeful attitude, the academic performance of externals can improve (Noel, Forsyth, & Kelley, 1987). By training oneself to change how we attribute causes to factors outside of our control to things we actually do control, then we can increase our internality (Shelton, Anastopoulos, & Linden, 1985).

Make your own goals and work toward those goals. Setting goals and fulfilling those goals through personal efforts can help to restructure our thinking and show us that our efforts can be fruitful and influential—helping us to achieve the outcomes that we want for our life.

Additionally, it creates a virtuous cycle by helping to build our sense of self-efficacy and self-confidence.

Practice making decisions and solving problems rather than avoiding them or handing them over to a third party to solve. This builds confidence and helps to strengthen our resourcefulness so that when adverse circumstances confront us, we are able to fight back through intelligent decision-making and problem solving.

By reading more, doing more practice, asking questions of teachers and others, we begin to take charge of our learning. Our attitudes and actions change as we begin to see the teacher as a resource for learning, rather than as the source of learning.

References

Abdullahi, O. E. (2000). Relationship among achievement motivation, Self-esteem, locus of control and academic performance of Nigerian University students. *The Nigerian Journal of Guidance and Counseling.* 7(1).122-131. (Journal of the University of Ilorin Department of Guidance and Counseling).

Adams, S. (2000, December 7). *The Impact of Religiosity and Locus of Control on Academic Achievement in College Students.*

Anderman, L. & Midgley, C. (1997). Motivation and middle school students. In J. L. Irvin (Ed.), *What current research says to the middle level practitioner* (pp. 41-48). Columbus, OH: National Middle School Association.

Basgall, J. A., & Snyder, C. R. (1988). Excuses in waiting: External locus of control and reactions to success-failure feedback. *Journal of Personality and Social Psychology, 54*(4), 656.

Boss, M. W., & Taylor, M. C. (1989). The relationship between locus of control and academic level and sex of secondary school students. *Contemporary Educational Psychology, 14*(4), 315-322.

Carden, R., Bryant, C., & Moss, R. (2004). Locus of control, test anxiety, academic procrastination, and achievement among college students 1. *Psychological reports, 95*(2), 581-582.

Edison Tech Center (2010). *History of the Incandescent Light (1802–Today)*, Retrieved December 5, 2012, from http://www.edisontechcenter.org/incandescent.html,

Findley, M. J., & Cooper, H. M. (1983). Locus of control and academic achievement: A literature review. Journal of Personality and Social Psychology; *Journal of Personality and Social Psychology, 44*(2), 419.

Gifford, D. D., Briceno-Perriott, J., & Mianzo, F. (2006). *Locus of Control.*

Grimes, P. W., Millea, M. J., & Woodruff, T. W. (2004). Grades—Who's to blame? Student evaluation of teaching and locus of control. *The Journal of Economic Education, 35*(2), 129-147.

King, L. (2006). Resilience, helplessness, control orientations, and set. In Conference paper.

Latu, V. F. (2004). There is more to learning mathematics than mathematics: Attributional beliefs and motivation of Maori and Pacific Island students. In *Mathematics education for the third millennium: Towards 2010*: Proceedings of the 27th annual conference of the Mathematics Education Research Group of Australasia, Townsville, 27th-30th June (Vol. 2, pp. 343-350).

Noel, J. G., Forsyth, D. R., & Kelley, K. N. (1987). Improving the performance of failing students by overcoming their self-serving attributional biases. *Basic and Applied Psychology, 8*, 151-162.

Pajares, F. (n.d). *Information on Self-Efficacy.* Retrieved December 5, 2012, from http://www.uky.edu/~eushe2/Pajares/self-efficacy.html

Seifert, T. (2004). Understanding student motivation. *Educational Research, 46*(2), 137-149.

Shelton, T. L., Anastopoulos, A. D., & Linden, J. D. (1985). An attribution training program with learning disabled children. *Journal of Learning Disabilities, 18*(5), 261-265.

Suh, S., & Suh, J. (2006). Educational Engagement and Degree Attainment among High School Dropouts. *Educational Research Quarterly, 29*(3), 11-20.

Thomas Alva Edison. (2012). *The Biography Channel website*. Retrieved 02:19, Dec 05, 2012, from http://www.biography.com/people/thomas-edison-9284349.

Thomas Edison Million Dollar Secrets of Invention (n.d.). Retrieved December 5, 2012, from http://www.wilywalnut.com/Fail-Fast-Success-Failure-Wonderful-Edison.html

Weiner, B. (1985). An attributional theory of achievement motivation and emotion. *Psychological review, 92*(4), 548.

Wolk, S. & D. Bloom. (1978). The Interactive Effects of Locus of Control and Situational Stress upon Performance Accuracy and Time. *Journal of Personality, 46*, 279-298.

LAW 3: TO ACHIEVE ACADEMIC SUCCESS YOU MUST BE MOTIVATED BY ACADEMIC SUCCESS.

Nothing in the world can take the place of Persistence. Talent will not; nothing is more common than unsuccessful men with talent. Genius will not; unrewarded genius is almost a proverb. Education will not; the world is full of educated derelicts. Persistence and determination alone are omnipotent. The slogan 'Press On' has solved and always will solve the problems of the human race.
—Calvin Coolidge

Motivation Makes Us Limitless

Some researchers are often bewildered about why certain students are more motivated than others are. There is no mystery here. The truth is that some students desire success, and the things that academic achievement allows, more than other students do. For the former students, their goals are non-negotiable. This, I offer, is the true meaning of being motivated: willingness and a determination to put everything, if necessary, on the line, and to persist in the face of opposition to achieve one's goals.

We see this truth evidenced in the story and history of Vietnam. Vietnam had a long and prolific history of colonization and liberation. For almost one millennium, they were ruled by the Chinese, winning independence in 938AD. In the mid-nineteenth century, the French would again colonize the nation, until the mid-twentieth century when the Geneva Accords of 1954 partitioned Vietnam into North and South, with Ho Chi Minh ruling North Vietnam under the aegis of the Democratic Republic of Vietnam, and Emperor Bao Dai ruling South Vietnam, heading the State of Vietnam party. This artificially imposed separation of Vietnam would lead to a twenty-year civil war called, unsurprisingly, the Vietnam War, which lasted from 1955 to 1975.

The commitment to victory by the North Vietnamese was strongly sounded in the development of the Ho Chi Minh trail, which articulated North and South Vietnam, meandering through Laos and Cambodia. It became the North Vietnamese complex supply line that would provide labor and raw materials to the Vietcong (National Front for the Liberation of South Vietnam) and the North Vietnamese Army (PAVN). The engineer corps that had responsibility to build and extend the trail had a simple motto, which captured their motivation, "Blood may flow, but the road will not stop" (Lamb, 2008). It was this similar attitude of unyielding goal-fixation that the highly trained and motivated PAVN demonstrated, in the tattoo that many sported, "Born in the North, to die in the South." This is to be compared against the consideration of many American soldiers: DEROS—Date of Expected Return from Overseas, as one site puts it, "The day all soldiers in Vietnam were waiting for." [2] DEROS promised the combatant a way out of the war other than a physical or psychological casualty (Kormos, 1978). It individualized the war and mitigated unit cohesion.

The United States vigorous and concerted efforts to derail the Ho Chi Minh trail construction through B-52 bombing, artillery shelling, burning forests, initiating landslides, denuding jungles, and burying sensors into the ground that communicated traffic data to neighboring US surveillance base were unsuccessful. The efforts failed to halt the construction as work continued and the infiltration of North Vietnamese into South Vietnam grew from some 1,800 in 1959 to 80,000 in 1968. The US National Security Agency's history of the war would later describe this trail as "one of the great achievements of military engineering of the 20th century" (Hanyok, 2002).

Achievement Motivation and Academic Performance

Motivation is often referred to as the degree of student engagement: how does the learner think and feel about education? What is the quality of her investment and attachment to learning? [Tucker, Zayco and Herman, 2002, p. 477]. So important is motivation that all other laws of academic success feed on this for operational performance, that is, on this runs all of the other laws [Tucker, et al.

2002]. Put more colloquially, if you aren't motivated, you aren't moving!

Motivation is a psychological force that can be strengthened or weakened. Its affect is seen in the quality of student engagement, and the application expended in understanding the subject under consideration. The strength of this psychological force is proportionate to the learner's desire for academic success and those things that academic success provides, and their belief in the likelihood of success (Dornyei, 2001). It is not just "pressing on," as Coolidge exhorts us, but believing that by pressing on victory, however it is defined, will be achieved. For some, victory may mean graduating from high school, college, or earning a doctorate. For others it may mean getting an A in a course or performing to the best of one's ability. Failure is not seen as an option. This is the quality of the encouragement advanced by the title of 50 Cent's debut rap album, "Get Rich Or Die Tryin'." [Disclaimer: The author does not encourage any illicit activity to garner wealth; otherwise, the die tryin' part might come first!]

To strengthen our motivation, we must organize our goals around interests that connect with our passion. Our goals must not only be realistic, but must be relatable: related to the mission and vision we have for our own lives—the areas in which our strengths and personal gifts find their most dominant expression and effectiveness. It is this drive to achieve and to continuously improve on the path toward self-actualization, which underscores all lasting academic achievement.

From the Prosaic to the Poetic

Probably no other poem captures the vitality of "motivation as not quitting" more than the poem reproduced below. All readers are encouraged to paste a copy of it in a conspicuous place, for meditation, reflection, and encouragement when intervening forces would seek to dissuade and discourage your onward movement toward

your goal.

Don't You Quit

When things go wrong, as they sometimes will,
When the road you're trudging seems all uphill,
When the funds are low and the debts are high,
And you want to smile, but you have to sigh,
When care is pressing you down a bit -
Rest if you must, but don't you quit.

Life is queer with its twists and turns,
As every one of us sometimes learns,
And many a fellow turns about
When he might have won had he stuck it out.
Don't give up though the pace seems slow -
You may succeed with another blow.

Often the goal is nearer than
It seems to a faint and faltering man;
Often the struggler has given up
When he might have captured the victor's cup;
And he learned too late when the night came down,
How close he was to the golden crown.

Success is failure turned inside out -
The silver tint in the clouds of doubt,
And you never can tell how close you are,
It might be near when it seems afar;
So stick to the fight when you're hardest hit -
It's when things seem worst that you must not quit.

—Author Unknown

Arousing and Maintaining Motivation

We get an important insight from the first law of motion, articulated by Sir Isaac Newton, arguably one of the greatest mathematicians of all times. He stated that objects in motion stay in motion, and objects at rest stay at rest. In other words, objects tend to resist attempts to change their state of motion. [3] For those of us who are at rest, it means that we need an "unbalanced force," a push in the right direction. Getting in the company of progressive thinkers and doers, motivational speakers, and immersing one's self in the biographies of champions can provide that psychological push and momentum to set challenging goals and to begin to plan and take concrete steps to achieve the same. The key is to begin, or in the language of Nike, to just do it! The law of motion tells us that once we start going, we won't stop unless we allow some intervening force to derail us, such as discouragement, distress, or temporary failure.

As we discussed in the previous chapter, we are motivated around a goal that is relevant, inspiring, and challenging. You must know what it is you want and why you want it. Find good reasons for achieving your goals: material reward, self-actualization, or becoming serviceable to family and friends. Picture yourself achieving the goal, and the feelings that this success would bring to you. Through visualization, you mentally embed the goal, and hasten its manifestation. Write and rewrite the goal. Visit it often, and it will build momentum in you to work toward it, and to not give up.

Motivation also requires you to be self-compassionate. Be a friend to yourself! Research indicates that when we give ourselves a break, and do not beat ourselves down ritualistically, then we lead healthier and more optimistic lives (Parker-Pope, 2011). This isn't about being indulgent, or letting yourself go, but it means dialing down the voices that would seek to self-flog and self-punish to the extent that one is always on edge. We all make mistakes: it's healthy to forgive ourselves and to promise ourselves to do better. Dr. Neff (2011), author of the book, "Self-compassion: Stop Beating Yourself Up and Leave Insecurity Behind", also encourages us to write a letter of support to ourselves. Although the jury is still out, there is suggestion that self-compassion may indeed help to reduce anxiety, depression, and stress.

As you track your progress toward your ultimate goal, you will see concretely where you are achieving your sub-goals. Celebrate the achievement of these intermediate goals. Reward yourself with a break, a few minutes of mental and/or physical relaxation. Have a treat. As the goals achieved increase in magnitude, the reward may be more substantial to include watching a movie, going for a trip, or purchasing a luxury item.

Part of rewarding yourself is also finding encouragement when circumstances are bearing down. This is where the dictum, "know thyself" is appropriate. What picks you up when you are down? What is a source of revival for your spirit in hard times? It may be that you have some favorite poems that challenge you in times of need, or some memory gems/verses that you rehearse, which strengthen your heart and mind, or you have a notebook of inspirational quotes that you read during class, or while on a bus or train. There are many sources for inspiration in these times: movies, music, lively friends/family members, or even a tour of comedic clips from YouTube. All of these are vehicles and resources that should be deployed when you need a "pick-me-up" for those times when a cloud or shadow seeks to come between you and your goal. This is why it is so important to have inspirational quotes in conspicuous spots in those spaces that you inhabit.

Sometimes injecting some variety in the routine can be a great way for keeping the force of motivation strengthened. Change your schedule; try to find a different way to do routine tasks. Learn how to cook chicken a different way. Write a letter with an actual pen and paper!

Visit some place you have never gone to before. Make it a game or challenge to find a fun way to do the task that you dread doing. Doing something new and different encourages us to be lifelong learners, and keeps us excited, in the zone of continuous learning and growing.

Finally, being and staying motivated is also about being and staying connected with family and friends. Engaging in healthy relationships and having support, strengthens motivation. One such important relationship is the mentor-student relationship. If you are able to cultivate a relationship with an academic or business mentor, this can be a source of information, counsel, encouragement, and motivation. A mentor can provide valuable feedback, and provide a quality of accountability that is important to help one to remain focused and to keep on track in the pursuit of one's goals.

References

First Battalion 50th Infantry Association (n.d.). *Vietnam Era War "Jargon"*. Retrieved December 6,2012 from http://www.ichiban1.org/html/history_glossary.htm#D

Dörnyei, Z. (2001). *Teaching and researching motivation.* Allyn & Bacon.

Hanyok, RJ. *Spartans in Darkness*. Washington DC: Center for Cryptographic History, NSA, 2002, p. 94.

Kormos, H. R. (1978). The Nature of Combat Stress. In C. A. Figley, *Stress Disorders among Vietnam Vets* (p. 356). London: Routledge.

Lamb, D. (2008, March). Revolutionary Road. *Smithsonian.com*. Retrieved from December 5, 2012 from http://www.smithsonianmag.com/travel/da-revolutionary-road.html?c=y&story=fullstory

Newton's First Law of Motion (n.d.). Retrieved December 6, 2012 from http://www.physicsclassroom.com/class/newtlaws/u2l1a.cfm

Neff, K. (2011). Self-compassion: Stop beating yourself up and leave insecurity behind. New York, NY: William Morrow.

Parker-Pope, T (2011, February). Go Easy on Yourself, a New Wave of Research Urges. *The New York Times*. Retrieved from http://www.nytimes.com

Tucker, C. M., Zayco, R. A., & Herman, K. C. (2002). Teacher and child variables as predictors of academic engagement among low-income African American children. *Psychology in the Schools, 39*(4), 477-488.

LAW 4: BE ANXIOUS ABOUT NOTHING IF YOU WANT TO ACHIEVE SOMETHING

Worrying does not empty tomorrow of its sorrow, it empties today of its strength.

—Corrie Ten Boom

Manage Stress To Do your Best On High-Stakes Tests

There is something about taking a test that flips us out: they can easily be caricatured as Judgment Day, especially for the unprepared soul. High stakes testing carries a psychological burden that can be exacerbated by placing a premium on peer and family pressures, or worrying about the contingency of life outcomes on test results. This chapter argues that worry and doubt must be exchanged with work and faith in order to achieve a higher-performing state of mind and being. Until we change our talk and thought from worry to an acceptance of our self-efficacy and our ability to perform, then we will be mired in mediocrity—achieving less than our potential.

Moral teachers, personal life coaches, and pop music icons enthusiastically agree on the refrain: Don't worry; be happy! T. Harv Eker (2005), author of the *Secrets of the Millionaire Mind*, makes it plain that we must reverse our negative thought patterns, surrender our inhibiting belief system, and adopt a frame of mind that affirms the outcomes we desire in our lives. This mental transformation, he argues, is the bed soil in which creative ideas and personal success are seeded.

Stephen Covey (1997), in his groundbreaking work the *7 Habits of Highly Effective People*, goes at the same issue in the first habit that he examines: Be proactive. Covey argues that life is not about what happens to us; rather, life congeals in the substance of the choices we make in the light of the stimuli acting upon us. He notes that there are two categories of folks: those who simply react to the daily trove of incidents, accidents and worldly demands; and those who pro-act.

The difference is important. Reactive people dwell in the areas of concern—areas over which they have little to no control: worrying about the weather, or acts of terrorism, or the national debt. To be reactive is ultimately to become disempowered and to surrender one's life design to the power of external chaotic events. Proactive persons, on the other hand, live in the circle of influence or areas of control. Proactive folks center their efforts on things over which they can exercise control, things they can change: their health, family, and work issues. By improving the things over which they have control, they seek to improve the quality of their lives. One mindset is problem seeking; the other mindset is solution seeking.

Good Stress vs. Bad Stress

In 1908, the psychologists Robert Yerkes and John Dodson formulated a relationship between arousal and performance.

This "law" offers that when an individual is undertaking a difficult or challenging intellectual task, then by increasing physiological arousal (i.e., task excitement or engagement) or mental stimulation (i.e., motivation or enthusiasm), one's performance may increase (i.e., a little stress is good). This lower level of arousal may be required to support the necessary amount of concentration for task-completion or goal-achievement.

Some tasks, however, may be more demanding and may require a greater degree of stamina or persistence, and this would be supported by encouraging higher levels of motivation. The law shows, however, that while some arousal may be initially energizing, too much arousal—in the form of high stress levels—can lead to tunnel vision, impaired memory, and ineffective problem-solving.

The Brain and Distress

Daniel Goleman, the godfather of emotional intelligence in popular folklore, unpacks for us the "biology of boredom, frazzle, and the brain's sweet spot for performance" (Goleman, 2006). He notes that brain research indicates that when we are frazzled, or overwhelmed by the daily upsets, that our thinking moves from being deliberate to seeking crisis management. This means that thoughtfulness and creativity are usurped by the need to respond quickly, and from an emotional rather than a rational executive center in the brain. This neuro-emotional reaction to daily hassles limits individual learning by handicapping the ability to take in new information. He further notes, "The more the pressure intensifies, the less able we are to hold information in working memory, to pay attention or to react flexibly—let alone creatively. The further we go down this arc, the greater our descent into cognitive dysfunction." In other words, a high level of stress mitigates against effective learning, or recall.

Goleman offers that for the best learning, students should be excited, challenged, and motivated by what they are learning. This stimulates the focus and the clarity requisite for effective and efficient learning. He notes that this corresponds to a neurochemical state of low adrenaline and cortisol levels, which promotes concentration or focus. High-stakes testing therefore induces a state of nervousness, which impairs cognitive function, and can lead to debilitating under-performance in concentration, learning, and recall. As Rose Kennedy, mother of John F. Kennedy, previewed decades before, "neither comprehension nor learning can take place in an atmosphere of anxiety."

Testing For Success

Our educational landscape is marked by a fixation with testing to measure the effectiveness of pedagogy, and the teachers' efficiency at delivering the curriculum in a manner consistent with meeting examination standards. The fixation with test performance leads to cognitive pressures on some test-takers who experience the immobilizing or heart-stopping effects of test anxiety. Some argue that the concern should be about engaging learners rather than teaching to the test (Saslow, 2008). Others argue that education should not be about subordinating learning to worrying over GPA status. Nevertheless, it does not change the reality that compulsory testing produces a level of stress and anxiety that some students must learn to cope with in order to perform well in formal educational settings.

While some amount of student stress can be sourced from authoritative others (stress from parents, teachers, or administrators), the high-stakes nature of tests may induce student-anxiety independent of environmental causes. Test anxiety is largely sourced through a fear of failure, and how such a possibility could affect one's sense of self as incompetent or less able. Stress is generally manifested in those situations where there is high demand for success accompanied with low control over outcomes. Unmanaged stress can easily lead to feelings of incompetence, and emotional upset in the form of discouragement or anger.

Learning to Relax

Managing test anxiety means developing certain strategic habits to cope with the challenges of the expected examination. The best antidote against worry is preparation, focusing on those areas over which we can exercise control. These include the following:

- First, make sure to find a good mix of places for regular studying.
- Second, during the season of preparation for examination, reduce unnecessary social and part-time

activities that may take away time from preparation, and effective focus on examination concentration.

- Third, develop a plan for the test or examination, which may include a timetable of revision activities, readings, working through past examination papers, and remediation intervention in the form of tutoring or teacher-assistance.

- Fourth, make sure that you are familiar with the format of the examination, the usual instructions and information that regulates the examination, what you are allowed to take in, and what you are not, as well as how questions will be organized.

- Fifth, practice relaxation techniques, get a good night's sleep, and visualize getting a good score. By slowing down, focusing on one thing at a time, and practicing the art of mindfulness—paying attention to the thing at hand, in the moment—we can improve our concentration and "build up neural real estate that is better able to deal with the variegated demands of the endlessly multitasking, infinitely connected world" (Konnikova, 2012).

- Finally, no matter what the outcome we must accept and believe that everything will work for our best, or, as Steve Jobs declared, that the dots will connect in the future.

References

Casbarro, J. (2005). Test Anxiety & what You Can Do about it: A Practical Guide for Teachers, Parents, and Kids. Dude Publishing.

Covey, S. R. (1997). The 7 habits of highly effective families. St. Martin's Press.

Eker, T. H. (2005). Secrets of the millionaire mind: Mastering the inner game of wealth. HarperBusiness.

Goleman, D. (2006). Emotional intelligence; why it can matter more than IQ. Bantam.

Goleman, D (2006, December 27). Aiming for the Brain's Sweet Spot. *The New York Times*. Retrieved from http://www.nytimes.com

Halpern, D. F., & Hakel, M. D. (2003). Applying the science of learning to the university and beyond: Teaching for long-term retention and transfer. *Change: The Magazine of Higher Learning, 35*(4), 36-41.

Howe, Michael J. A., & Davidson J. W., & Sloboda, J. A. (1998) Innate Talents: Reality Or Myth. *Behavioural and Brain Sciences* 21 399-442.

Konnikova, M. (2012, December 15). The Power of Concentration. *The New York Times*. Retrieved from http://www.nytimes.com

Saslow, L (2008, January 20). Offering Fresh Weapons Against Test Anxiety. *The New York Times*. Retrieved from http://www.nytimes.com

Text of Steve Jobs' Commencement address (2005). (n.d.). Retrieved from http://news.stanford.edu/news/2005/june15/jobs-061505.html

Yerkes R. M., Dodson J. D. (1908). The relation of strength of stimulus to rapidity of habit-formation. *Journal of Comparative Neurology and Psychology,* 18, 459-482.

LAW 5: THE LAW OF GOAL-SETTING—TO ACHIEVE BIG, WE MUST DREAM BIG

If you want to be happy, set a goal that commands your thoughts, liberates your energy, and inspires your hopes.
—Andrew Carnegie

It is not enough to take steps, which may someday lead to a goal; each step must be itself a goal and a step likewise.
—Johann Wolfgang von Goethe

The Race to the Moon

It was a warm fall afternoon, in Rice University Stadium, Houston Texas when President John F. Kennedy took to the podium in September 1962, and reframed the mission to colonize space. At that time, the USSR was well ahead in the space race, being the first nation to launch a satellite into orbit (October 4, 1957), and the first to send a man into orbit around Earth (Yuri Gagarin, 12 April, 1961). By mid-1961, the USA had chalked up a total of five minutes of piloted flight in space.

Kennedy, stirring to the historical demands of the time, spoke passionately to the stadium audience and boldly articulated a clear goal and an explicit timeline for the American scientific community. He declared:

We choose to go to the moon in this decade and do the other things, not because they are easy, but because they are hard, because that goal will serve to organize and measure the best of our energies and skills, because that challenge is one that we are willing to accept, one we are unwilling to postpone, and one which we intend to win.

The goal was clear, ambitious, and worthy of a nation that dared to be a leader among nations. Kennedy committed America to land a man on the moon, to bring him back to Earth safely, and to do all of this before the end of the decade. The focus of this commitment and goal galvanized the energies of over two million people, with both blood and treasure being spent in the process.

Appropriately, the Apollo 11 would launch on July 16, 1969 from the Kennedy Space Center, with Commander

Neil Armstrong, command module pilot Michael Collins, and lunar module pilot Edwin "Buzz" Aldrin. Some one million spectators witnessed the launch on site and from the neighboring environs, with 600 million people by television. By July 20, 1969, Neil Armstrong would take that fateful step for humankind, onto the surface of the moon. Kennedy's vision was accomplished with some five months to spare.

Goal-Setting and Academic Performance

Does it matter if we set goals? Can setting goals affect academic performance and achievement? What if we simply rely on the goals that our parents or teachers set for us: is that better than setting our own goals? Is it better if our goal is to master a topic, or simply to get a good grade?

One of the habits of effective living, as articulated by Covey (1997), and recognized by others, is the importance of living with the endgame in front view. As nineteenth century French philosopher Victor Cousin urges, "In everything the ends well defined are the secret of durable success." We must identify the final desired state, and work backward to where we are, to identify the intermediary steps required to take us to the ultimate goal. In this way, our lives are purposefully organized around goals rather than spent and dissipated on the pleasures of our diverse drives. Taylor (1964), in doing a review of the literature spanning the period 1933 through 1963, found that there was a significant discrepancy between the goals of achievers and underachievers. The goals of underachievers were non-existent or unrealistic, while the goals of achievers were relevant, realistic, and achievable. Taylor concluded that one of the determinants of student achievement is setting realistic goals.

It is not merely that having goals matter, but personally setting them is also important. Hannafin (1981) elaborated on this finding. He noted that when students set their own goals, they achieved more of them than when teachers set them. Those who set their own goals reported improvements in their skill to set goals relative to those who had them set by teachers. Dale Schunk (1985) reported that when students were involved in goal setting that it improves the students' learning and their self-efficacy.

Setting realistic goals, and being involved in the setting of those goals, not only builds student confidence, and enables learning to take place, but also encourages and facilitates student achievement. This conclusion is supported by a number of researchers (Arlin 1975; Rosswork, 1977; Wang & Stiles, 1967; Gagne, Bing, & Bing, 1977; Gagne & Rothkopf, 1975; Locke, et al., 1981).

Setting your own goals and achieving those goals turns out to have several important spillover benefits. It improves student engagement (i.e., more time is spent on the task in the classroom, Sagotsky, Patterson and Lepper, 1978) and improves student interest in the subject being learned by building students' sense of self-efficacy (Zimmerman, et al. 1992). This sense of achievement and self-efficacy enhances intrinsic motivation. Goal-setting and goal-achievement increases the student's understanding of her role in the learning process, builds responsibility for achieving learning outcomes, and makes learning more meaningful. As students grow in their sense of self-efficacy, they tend to set more challenging goals, and this tends to lead to greater levels of academic achievement (Wood & Locke, 1987).

From the above discussion, it is clear that setting goals is important, along with the process involved in the setting of those goals. Another important factor in academic achievement is the nature and number of goals that are set. Is your goal to get the best possible grade in your economics class? Alternatively, is it to understand what economics is about and the role of economic agency in the organization of society and in individual decision-making? Alternatively, is your goal simply to pass the course with as little pain as possible?

Recent research indicates that learners who seek to get good grades **as well as** who seek to understand the subject matter do much better than those who only have one achievement in focus: whether that achievement is passing the course, learning the material, or getting a good grade. These types of students not only have the highest self-efficacy (Pintrich & Garcia, 1991), but they are able to achieve more academically (Archer, 1994; Bouffard et al. 1995; Roebken, 2007). Roebken, reviewing survey responses from some 2300 students across all 8 campuses of the University of California, reported that students with the multiple goals of doing well and understanding the subject matter are not only more satisfied with their school experience, but achieve better grades, combine learning from different courses more regularly, apply more effort, and collaborate more often with their peers to understand better the coursework when compared to those who only had a single-type of goal.

Therefore, Roebken underscores for us that it is about not only setting goals, but also setting the right types of goals and setting multiple goals, which will encourage the application of complex learning strategies, additional time in the preparation for classes, and more active involvement in the class. Having multiple achievement goals helps students to be more flexible and successful across the learning environments they encounter (Roebken, 2007; Valle et al, 2003). As chapters 12 and 13 will further develop, students who set goals to master and to perform well, and who support this by deliberate practice (i.e., monitoring performance and using feedback to consistently improve) tend to have a higher GPA (Plant, et. al, 2005).

Being Smart About Goal-Setting

What then should be your pattern for goal setting and goal-achievement? The first principle is that you must have the end clearly defined, that is, you must clearly understand what learning outcomes you would like to achieve and what performance or grade outcome you would like to earn. This visualization of the ends is the blueprint that will guide the physical creation of these goals. This approach should inform how every day, course, or project is executed: where am I going? How can I best get there? Research indicates that specific goals carry far more psychological force than general ones, and provide the learner a clear benchmark against which to gauge performance and achievement (Locke & Bryan, 1969; Rosswork, 1977). Specific goals answer three particular questions: What am I going to do? Why is this goal personally important? How am I going to achieve this goal (Arina, 2010)? Not only should you work through these questions but also you should write down your answers, and create a vision board to go along with your goals. By having these words and images in a conspicuous place where we can daily see them and read them, they increase commitment and focus and are more likely to take on flesh and walk into our lives.

The second principle is that our goals must be measurable: we should know without any hesitation whether we are hitting or missing the target goals. In other words, the process of specificity carries in it a measurable criterion. Not only must the outcome be measurable, but the time for achieving the outcome must be measurable as well. The goal of losing five pounds of weight in one month may mean spending fifteen minutes jogging every day. Not only is the ultimate goal measurable (five pounds weight loss in one month) but the intermediate daily goals are also measurable (fifteen minutes of daily exercise). By providing goals that are measurable, we can then manage our thinking and our doing, and guide both toward achieving the desired outcomes. Learners can use the feedback that they receive from tests, assignments and other assessment exercises to know whether they are achieving or falling short of the desired goals, to update efforts (Arlin, 1975; Erez, 1977).

The third principle of effective goal setting and goal-achievement is that the goal must be attainable (i.e., it must be a realistic goal). This does not mean that the goal should not be challenging: but every (challenging) goal should be do-able and capable of being broken down into manageable and achievable daily, weekly, and monthly sub-goals. It must be the case also that the learner believes in his or her ability to achieve the ultimate goal, otherwise commitment will weaken and focus will fade. Another interpretation of attainability is that you should be economical in the number of goals that you set. Do not set many goals, as this too will have the same effect as setting unrealistic goals: weakening your effort, and eventually causing loss of focus.

In conclusion, we see that for effective goal setting and goal-achievement, we must have clearly defined goals, they must be challenging and achievable, and they must be measurable.

References

Archer, J. (1994). Achievement goals as a measure of motivation in university students. *Contemporary Educational Psychology*, 19, 430-446.

Arina (2010, February 20). SMART Goal-Setting: A Surefire Way To Achieve Your Goals. *Goal Setting Guide*. Retrieved December 6, 2012 from http://www.goal-setting-guide.com

Arlin, P. (1975). Cognitive development in adulthood: A fifth stage? *Developmental Psychology,* 11, 602-606

Bandura, A. (1977). Self-efficacy: Toward a unifying theory of behavioral change. *Psychological Review*, 84, 191-215.

Bandura, A. (1986). Social foundations of thought and action: A social cognitive theory. Englewood Cliffs, NJ: Prentice-Hall.

Bouffard, T., Boisvert, J., Vezeau, C., & Larouche, C. (1995). The impact of goal orientation on self-regulation and performance among college students. *British Journal of Educational Psychology*, 65(3), 317-329.

Dweck, C. (1999). Kerr, B. (1997). *Smart Girls* (Revised). Dayton, OH: Ohio Psychology Press.

Dweck, C. S. (1975). The role of expectations and attributions in the alleviation of learned helplessness. *Journal of Personality and Social Psychology*, 31, 674-685.

Elliot, Andrew (2006, June 1). The Hierarchical Model of Approach-Avoidance Motivation. *Motivation and Emotion*, 30(2): 111-116. doi:10.1007/s11031-006-9028-7

Erez, M. (1977). Feedback: A necessary condition for the goal setting-performance relationship. *Journal of Applied Psychology, 62*(5), 624.

Gagne, E. D. & Rothkopf, E. Z. (1975). Text organization and learning goals. *Journal of Educational Psychology*, 67, 445-50.

Gagné, E. D., Bing, S. B., Bing, J. R. (1977, August). *Journal of Educational Psychology, 69*(4), 428-431. doi: 10.1037/0022-0663.69.4.428

Graham, S., & Barker, G. P. (1990). The down side of help: An attribution-developmental analysis of helping behavior as a low-ability cue. *Journal of Educational Psychology*, 82, 7-14.

Hannafin, M. J. (1981). Effects of teacher and student goal setting and evaluations on mathematics achievement and student attitudes. *The Journal of Educational Research*, 321-326.

Kazdin, A. E. (1974). Comparative effects of some variations of covert modeling. *Journal of Behavior Therapy and Experimental Psychiatry*, 5, 225-231.

Kazdin, A. E. (1975). Covert modeling, imagery assessment, and assertive behavior. *Journal of Consulting and Clinical Psychology*, 43, 716-724.

Locke, E. A., Shaw, K. N., Saari, L. M., & Latham, G. P. (1981). Goal setting and task performance: 1969–1980. *Psychological bulletin, 90*(1), 125.

McAuley, E. (1985). Modeling and self-efficacy: A test of Bandura's model. *Journal of Sport Psychology*, 7, 283-295.

Meichenbaum, D. H. (1971). Examination of model characteristics in reducing avoidance behavior. *Journal of Personality and Social Psychology*, 17, 298-307.

Plant, A. E., Ericsson, K. A., Hill, L., & Asberg, A. (2005). Why study time does not predict grade point average across college students: implications of deliberate practice for academic performance. *Contemporary Educational Psychology*, 30, 96-116.

Pintrich, P. R., & Garcia, T. (1991). Student goal orientation and self-regulation in the college classroom. *Advances in motivation and achievement: Goals and self-regulatory processes*, 7 (371-402).

Pintrich, P. R., & De Groot, E. V. (1990). Motivational and self-regulated learning components of classroom academic performance. *Journal of educational psychology*, *82*(1), 33.

Plant, E. A., Ericsson, K. A., Hill, L., & Asberg, K. (2005). Why study time does not predict grade point average across college students: Implications of deliberate practice for academic performance. *Contemporary Educational Psychology*, *30*(1), 96-116.

Roebken, H. (2007). The influence of goal orientation on student satisfaction, academic engagement and achievement. *Electronic Journal of Research in Educational Psychology, 5*(3), 679-704.

Rosswork, S. G. (1977). Goal setting: The effects on an academic task with varying magnitudes of incentive. *Journal of Educational Psychology*, *69*(6), 710.

Sagotsky, G., Patterson, C. J., & Lepper, M. R. (1978). Training children's self-control: A field experiment in self-monitoring and goal-setting in the classroom. *Journal of Experimental Child Psychology*, *25*(2), 242-253.

Schefter, James (1999). *The Race: The uncensored story of how America beat Russia to the Moon.* New York: Doubleday. ISBN 0-385-49253-7.

Schunk, D. H. (1984). Sequential attributional feedback and children's achievement behaviors. *Journal of Educational Psychology*, 75, 511-518.

Schunk, D. H. (1985). Self? efficacy and classroom learning. *Psychology in the Schools*, *22*(2), 208-223.

Schunk, D. H., & Hanson, A. R. (1985). Peer models: Influence on children's self-efficacy and achievement. *Journal of Educational Psychology*, 77, 313-322.

Schunk, D. H., & Rice, J. M. (1984, August). *Strategy self-verbalization: Effects on remedial readers' comprehension and self-efficacy*. Paper presented at the annual meeting of the American Psychological Association. Toronto, Canada.

Taylor, R. G. (1964). Personality traits and discrepant achievement: A review. *Journal of Counseling Psychology*, 11, 76-82.

Time Management Success (n.d.). Retrieved December 6, 2012 from http://www.time-management-success.com/student-goal-setting.html

Valle, A., Cabanach, R. G., Núñez, J. C., González-Pienda, J., Rodríguez, S., & Pineiro, I. (2003). Cognitive, motivational, and volitional dimensions of learning: An empirical test of a hypothetical model. *Research in Higher Education*, *44*(5), 557-580.

Wang, M. C., & Stiles, B. (1976). An investigation of children's concept of self-responsibility for their school learning. *American Educational Research Journal*, *13*(3), 159-179.

Wood, R. E., & Locke, E. A. (1987). The relationship of self-efficacy and grade goals to academic performance. *Educational and Psychological Measurement*, 47, 1013-1024.

Zimmerman, B. J., & Martinez-Pons, M. (1990). Student differences in self-regulated learning: Relating grade, sex, and giftedness to self-efficacy and strategy use. *Journal of Educational Psychology, 82,* 51-59.

Zimmerman, B. J., Bandura, A., Martinez-Pons, M. (1992). Self-motivation for academic attainment: The role of self-efficacy beliefs and personal goal setting. *American Educational Research Journal, 29*(3), 663-676.

LAW 6: THE LAW OF ENGAGEMENT— THERE CAN BE NO GREAT ACHIEVEMENT WITHOUT GREAT COMMITMENT

Once a man has made a commitment to a way of life, he puts the greatest strength in the world behind him. It's something we call heart power. Once a man has made this commitment, nothing will stop him short of success.

—Vincent Lombardi

Changing the world in 9.58 seconds

He is called 'The Beast,' a moniker given to him by his training partner, Usain Bolt. The world knows Usain Bolt: possibly the greatest, most marketable, and most loved athlete of all times. However, who is Yohan 'the Beast' Blake? One can easily be forgiven for his unrecognizability before his grand performance on the global arena in the World Championships in Daegu, when he collared the 100m title after Usain bolted before the starter's gun was fired.

Very few people have ever defeated Bolt. He carries an aura of invincibility—reminiscent of Iron Mike Tyson, in his heyday as the then undisputed world heavyweight boxing champion. Blake, however, is one of the few persons to have defeated Bolt, and is the only person to have done so *twice*, shutting out Bolt in the Jamaican National Trials from both the 100m and 200m pole positions in June 2012. Bolt telegraphed as much in an interview in 2008 when he was asked which athlete could challenge him, "Watch out for Yohan Blake. He works like a beast. He's there with me step for step in training" (Turnbull, 2012)

In 2008, Blake was only 18, and was not a member of the Jamaican Olympic squad going to Beijing. Two years earlier, he was fourth in the World Junior Championships. Blake's rise to international stardom, under the tutelage of world-beating coach Glen Mills, was preceded by an austere training regime to which he committed himself.

"Why do they call me The Beast?" Blake says. "Because even when we have breaks I still train. On Christmas break, coach Mills has to call and say, 'You are on a break. You need to take some rest.' "That is how I work. When you guys are sleeping at night, I am out there working. That's why they call me The Beast. I work twice as hard as everybody else" (Turnbull, 2012).

As the Italian-American Champion Racing Driver, Mario Andretti, once said, "Desire is the key to motivation, but its determination and commitment to an unrelenting pursuit of your goal—a commitment to excellence—that will enable you to attain the success you seek."

Student Engagement

Commitment matters. The manner in which we approach school cultures our attitudes to real-world responsibilities: work, family, and, recreation. The ability to engage life emotionally, intellectually, and physically demonstrates a holistic rather than a skewed response to the life demands we all face. Student engagement is therefore, succinctly, or briefly, a skill for life, or, in the words of Kuh (2009), it is a quality that "builds the foundations of skills and dispositions people need to live a productive, satisfying life after college."

What do we mean by 'student engagement'? Students engage their studies at two primary levels. First, there is an intellectual engagement. This involves attendance to lessons, participation in lessons, preparation for lessons, and completion of homework activities. Second, there is a social engagement. This refers to the extra-curricular involvement of students in the clubs etc., and their interactions with other students.

Engagement means that the student is no longer a spectator to his learning, but actively involved in the process of learning and understanding—constructing knowledge. The emotional byproducts are apparent: enjoyment and resilience. As one oft quoted Chinese proverb states, "Tell me and I'll forget; show me and I may remember; involve me and I'll understand." The process of engagement helps to secure greater purchase on the taught content.

Mind Where You Sit

While you can have achievement without engagement, and engagement without achievement, the two tend to be positively correlated. There is no better illustration of this in the literature than the relationship between where a student sits (or prefers to sit) and proximity to the teacher. Research indicates that where a student sits influences the amount of attention that he or she receives from the speaker, and mutually, how much attention is paid to the speaker.

A number of research findings support the claim that students who sit at the front of the class outperform their back-seat-minded counterparts. This, of course, assumes students are attending lectures—a good thing to do, since research evidence suggests that being absent diminishes the student's ability to understand the material (Topping, 1994).

While the most scholarly, learning-motivated, and outgoing students will be readily inclined to sit at or near the front of the class—the benefits of this highly interactional zone can flow to all of those who seek to take advantage of it. The benefits from this learning-rich zone stem from the following features.

Closeness to the speaker facilitates greater engagement by students with the speaker. It increases the likelihood of being asked questions, and the ability to respond to questions. Proximity improves access to the audio-visual resources deployed in the teaching moment (i.e., students can better hear and see what the teacher is doing). This encourages greater participation, improved note taking, and consistent class attendance. The rapport and participation in class has a motivational dimension, which can fuel greater resilience, and abet or encourage preparation for lectures. This creates a virtuous cycle, and enhances a favorable outlook by the student on the course.

Sitting near the front helps to improve attentiveness—this may be because proximity increases the sense of accountability to the teacher, or plays upon the student's academic courtesies as she seeks not to be rude by dint of inattentiveness. This is, therefore, prime real estate for those students who suffer easily from the distractions of peers, social media networks, or shyness / timidity.

If by sitting closer to the teacher, a student is encouraged to participate more in class, then this can stimulate the development of higher order thinking skills. Active engagement in the learning experience by students has been shown by the research to positively influence student learning.

The cultivation of a relationship with the teacher/lecturer is a critical ingredient in encouraging student engagement and motivation. Dwelling in this high interaction zone can help to build this relationship and thus feed into improved academic achievement. Teachers can more easily observe if something is wrong, and, thus, respond to the learner's needs. When students see firsthand that a teacher cares, this can strengthen engagement and commitment to study.

Promoting Engagement

It is clear that just telling a person to "be more engaged" does not solve the problem of low engagement. It is hoped that the above discussion provides a practical and actionable step: move closer to the front of the class. Understandably, not everyone can sit near the front of the class. **However,** everyone can have a front-seat personality and preference. Everyone can desire to be near the front. This matters. It demonstrates a desire to be engaged in learning.

Even if one's heart is not into attending classes, neither into sitting near the front of the class, the truth is that just as the heart and mind influences the body, the body can also influence the mind and the heart. What does this mean? The answer lies in the popular dictum, "fake it until you make it." Join the club. Participate more in class. Sit at the front of the class. Amy Cuddy, professor and researcher of nonverbal behavior at Harvard, improves on the dictum, urging, "fake it until you become it." Her insight is that our body language not only influences how others see us, but also how we see ourselves. We can move from the external to the internal. Engage with the body. As the body engages, the mind changes. Changes in the mind will change behavior. Felicitously, behavior changes outcomes and paves the road for success.

References

Cuddy, A. (2012, June). *Amy Cuddy: Your Body Language Shapes Who You Are* [Video File]. Retrieved from http://www.ted.com/talks/amy_cuddy_your_body_language_shapes_who_you_are.html

Kuh, G. D. (2009). What student affairs professionals need to know about student engagement. *Journal of College Student Development, 50*(6), 683-706.

Topping, E. (1994). The Effects of Absences on Performance in Principles of Macroeconomics.

Missouri Academy of Science Annual Meeting, Cape Girardeau, Missouri.

Turnbull, S. (2012, July 3). Meet Yohan Blake, the Beast who is driving Usain Bolt nuts—Athletics—More Sports. *The Independent*. Retrieved 2012-08-14.

Law 7: Self-Discipline Opens the Door to Academic Achievement

Mental toughness is many things and rather difficult to explain. Its qualities are sacrifice and self-denial. Also, most importantly, it is combined with a perfectly disciplined will that refuses to give in. It's a state of mind-you could call it character in action.

—Vince Lombardi

Your life in a Marshmallow

It is 1968 and you are a four-year-old child. Your supervising adult has just left you in a closet-like room sitting in front of a table with marshmallows, pretzels, and cookies on it. He has promised that you can have two treats instead of one if you wait until he returns; or you can ring a bell anytime and he will return and you can have a single treat. What do you do? Sit on your hands, look away, cover your eyes; try to resist as best as you can; or, grab it as soon as he is out of earshot or eyeshot, possibly sneaking a lick on the cream in-between the cookies?

If you are like any of those 653 children who sat at that table, about seven out of ten times you would fail to resist the power of the cookie. It turned out that roughly a third of the four-year olds would successfully resist. Another third would try to, but fail at different times in the experiment. The final third would just go for it—bell or no bell.

Fourteen years later, Walter Mischel, the researcher in charge of the experiment, would gather data on those who participated—with profound consequences. The analysis of the data showed that for the children who waited the brunt of the fifteen minutes the adult was away, that this decision was a strong predictor of life and academic success. Those who were able to delay gratification were more successful socially, academically, and emotionally. Those who did not successfully defer gratification suffered low self-esteem, had difficulty paying attention, tended to experience trouble at home and school, and were not able to maintain friendships (Marshmallows and Grit, n.d.; Lehrer, 2009) [4].

The conclusion of this famous test, called the Stanford Marshmallow Test, was that the ability to defer gratification through self-discipline was a major predictor of academic accomplishment. Though the experiment has been replicated several times, the original is considered "one of the most successful behavioral experiments" (Camber, 2008).

Michel argues that the important insight coming out of the experiment is that the kids had to figure out a way to make the situation work for them, to successfully delay gratification. They had to change the way they thought about the immediate world (Lehrer, 2009). In other words, they had to engage their minds or attention with something other than the treat in front of them—covering their eyes, playing hide-and-seek under the table, or singing a song (Lehrer, 2009).

Self-discipline and Academic Achievement

In another longitudinal study, one of 140 eighth graders in the first year, and an expanded study of 164 eighth graders in the following year, psychologists Angela Duckworth and Martin Seligman would report results that would also echo through the popular press: a major reason for students failing to realize their true intellectual potential lay in their failure to exercise self-discipline (Duckworth & Selgman, 2005).

Indeed, their findings went further—self-discipline [5] mattered more than academic competence (i.e., IQ) in predicting academic success. This supports work by Wolfe and Johnson (1995) who found that of thirty-two personality variables investigated (including self-esteem, extraversion, and energy level) self-discipline better predicted GPA than SAT scores. As Duckworth (2011) would years later write, "the capacity to govern ourselves effectively in the face of temptation has profound benefits across every major domain of life functioning."

Indeed self-discipline is a critical component in a student's social and emotional intelligence [6]. Piggybacking on the landmark book by Daniel Goleman in 1996, *Emotional Intelligence: Why It Can Matter More Than IQ* many schools and educational districts have introduced the teaching of social and emotional intelligence alongside the academic curriculum with key research findings indicating that the development of this skill improves academic performance (Six Seconds, 2007). Not only does academic accomplishment improve, but students' self-awareness, self-confidence, and empathy are also developed (Goleman, n.d.).

Developing Self-Control

Duckworth and Seligman argue that any program that can help students deny short-term pleasure to gain long-term rewards may be "the royal road to building academic achievement." Mischel advises us that once "you realize that will power is just a matter of learning how to control your attention and thoughts, you can really begin to increase it" (Lehrer, 2009). Indeed, there are a host of mental strategies that are available to strengthen the development of self-control.

Those who would be independent learners, and who seek to maximize their learning outcomes understand the importance of setting goals, striving after goals, and monitoring their achievement of those goals. This awareness of self in the process of learning is critical to achieving the goals of self-regulated learning, or crudely, independent learning.

Self-control figures prominently in the process of goal striving; that is, after we set our goals we require self-control to make progress to accomplishing those goals, in the face of obstacles that present themselves. How do we overcome those obstacles? We must develop our capacity to control ourselves. Steps to do so are delineated below.

First, find a hobby doing something you enjoy. Self-control can be thought of as a psychological muscle, which is built up by engaging in enjoyable activities in which the reward requires perseverance or the postponement of immediate gratification. Having personal projects that require significant time thinking about them, and completing them, also helps to strengthen this muscle. (Self-Regulation Supports Student Learning and Achievement, 2009). If the hobby is enjoyable, like playing chess or making YouTube videos, dopamine is released. This enhances learning while simultaneously inhibiting the secretion of stress hormones, which builds anxiety and impedes learning (Aamodt & Wang, 2012).

Second, engage in self-talk. Self-talk is a powerful tool, which can be deployed to encourage ourselves to remain committed to striving after the goal, and to exercise patience in the midst of contradictions and disappointments in our circumstances. Self-talk that motivates and guides actions can help us to maintain attention and to improve performance (Self-Regulation Supports Student Learning and Achievement, 2009). There are a variety of types of self-talk: **mastery self-talk** (I persuade myself to apply more effort so that I can know more and approach expert-like status); **performance relative ability self-talk** (I tell myself I should do as well or better than others in my class); and, **performance extrinsic self-talk** (I tell myself to keep studying and working because it will help to improve my grades) (Gonzalez et al., 2005).

Third, distract your mind or shift your attention by using "cognitive transformation." This is a mental trick where we think of the object of temptation as something less than desirable. So, for example, in the marshmallow test, we could think of the marshmallow as a cloud, a sponge, a small pillow, or any other similar article. Children who were taught this found that their staying and resisting power increased (Self-Regulation Supports Student Learning and Achievement, 2009).

Fourth, train your attention. There are several different strategies available to encourage this. These include expanding your visual awareness of what is happening in your environment; watching and listening for details; solving puzzles of various degrees of difficulty; and, *listening* to digital books of various complexities.

Fifth, participate regularly in a fitness or physical training activity. Regular exercise promotes self-control. High achievers normally engage in regular physical conditioning. Aerobic exercise is beneficial for enhancing prefrontal cortex activity, which contributes to cognitive flexibility, a feature of self-control. Practices such as yoga, martial arts, and meditation can be effective ways of building attention-maintaining skills through concentrated action upon the body and mind.

Sixth, apply self-consequences. The use of self-consequences as a motivational strategy has been found to be highly effective. In this strategy, we simply promise ourselves that we can do something fun or enjoyable later if we complete an assignment, do some reading/studying, or perform some activity that enables us to achieve our academic goals.

Seventh, reduce distractions in your environment. This strengthens mental clarity. Effectively, it may mean removing the television or game console, or whatever object may too easily interfere with sustained concentration. Alternatively, it may mean studying during the night when it is quieter, or in a location where the noise is low. Additionally, eating and drinking in preparation for study concentrates the mind by fending off hunger and thirst, and thus promotes physical alertness (Gonzalez et al., 2005).

Eighth, learn a second language. Mental flexibility is strengthened when one learns a second language. Mental flexibility is a facet of self-control. If one speaks more than one language, a decision must always be made as to which language to speak so that the hearer understands. Capacity at two languages helps to better comprehend abstract rules, or to ignore conflicting cues like the word green painted on a yellow card (Aamodt & Wang, 2012).

Finally, combine mental contrasting with implementation intentions. Research indicates that when these two strategies are combined, they yield superior results in improving self-discipline. So what does this mean? In mental contrasting, one thinks deeply, clearly, and vividly about the desired future in which the goal is achieved: passing a course with A+, graduating with a certain honor or GPA, or whatever other personal or academic goal one is striving toward. This is then contrasted with the obstacles present in your current situation. Therefore, you are bringing together in your thoughts what you want your future to look like, and what your current lived reality actually is. Duckworth et al. (2011), citing Oettingen et al., (2009), argue that the "simultaneous activation of the desired future and present reality emphasizes the necessity for action. When expectations of success are high, mental contrasting energizes individuals to take action and strengthens their goal commitment."

This strategy is coupled with an implementation intentions strategy, which takes the form of a series of if-then statements, which promote goal-achievement. For example, if the goal is to get a good grade in a course, and the most critical risk is feeling too lazy or distracted to spend enough time studying, then a set of implementation intentions could be, "If my favorite show comes on television I will grab my book remote instead of my television remote"; "If my friends call me while I am studying and want to gossip or chat, I will tell them they can help me to get better grades by calling back when I am done studying." An implementation intention then links some obstacle that may derail your chances of achieving your goals, with a response that will help you to overcome that obstacle [7] (Duckworth et al., 2011).

References

Aamodt, S. & S. Wang (2012, February 17). Building Self-Control the American Way. *The New York Times*. Retrieved from http://www.nytimes.com

Camber, Rebecca (2008, November 2). Marshmallow test—How resisting a sweet can lead to a better life. *Daily Mail*. Archived from the original on October 4, 2011. Retrieved October 4, 2011.

Duckworth, A. L., Grant, H., Loew, B., Oettingen, G., & Gollwitzer, P. M. (2011). Self-regulation strategies improve self-discipline in adolescents: benefits of mental contrasting and implementation intentions. *Educational Psychology,31*(1), 17-26.

Duckworth, A. L., & Seligman, M. E. (2005). Self-discipline outdoes IQ in predicting academic performance of adolescents. *Psychological Science, 16*(12), 939-944.

Duckworth, A. L. (2011). The significance of self-control. *Proceedings of the National Academy of Sciences, 108*(7), 2639-2640.

Goleman, D. (n.d.). *Emotional Intelligence*. Retrieved December 6, 2012 from http://danielgoleman.info/topics/emotional-intelligence/

Gonzalez, S., Dowson, M., Brickman, S. J., & McInerney, D. M. (2005). Self-regulation of academic motivation: advances in structure and measurement.

Lehrer, J (2009, May 18). Don't! *The New Yorker*. Retrieved December 6, 2012 from http://www.newyorker.com/.

Marshmallows and Grit. (n.d.). Retrieved from http://www.princetonacademy.org/weblogs/heads-journal/archives/Images/Microsoft%20Word%20-%20Olen's%20letter.pdf

Mayer, J. D. & Salovey, P. (1997). What is emotional intelligence? In Salovey, P., and Sluyter, D. (eds). *Emotional Development and Emotional Intelligence: Implications for Educators.* Basic Books, New York: pp. 3-31.

Moffitt T. E., et al., (2011). A gradient of childhood self-control predicts health, wealth, and public safety. *Proceedings of the National Academy of Science USA* 108, 2693-2698.

Oettingen, G., Mayer, D., Sevincer, A. T., Stephens, E.J., Pak, H., & Hagenah, M. (2009).

Mental contrasting and goal commitment: The mediating role of energization. *Personality and Social Psychology Bulletin, 35*, 608-622.

Self-Regulation Supports Student Learning and Achievement. (2009, May 26). Retrieved December 6, 2012 from http://clerestorylearning.blogspot.co.uk/2009/05/self-regulation-supports-student.html

Six Seconds (2007). A Case for Emotional Intelligence in Our Schools. www6seconds.org

Wolfe, R. N., & Johnson, S. D. (1995). Personality as a predictor of college performance. *Educational and Psychological Measurement*, 55, 177-185.

CHAPTER 8: THE LAW OF COLLABORATION—LEARNING OCCURS IN COMMUNITY

Learning is a social process that occurs through interpersonal interaction within a corporative context. Individuals working together construct shared understanding and knowledge.

—David Johnson, Roger Johnson and Karl Smith

Social contagion

Dan Ariely, in his book *The (Honest) Truth about Dishonesty*, develops his thesis that deceit in ourselves and in others is encouraged by the fabric of the social community of which we are a part. Ariely, a professor of psychology and behavioral economics, draws heavily on the much-disputed theory of social contagion: that people are more likely to be deceitful if they find that the communities in which they move facilitate deceit. In other words, deceit is infectious. Drawing from examples in the popular culture, he expands upon his claim that once a society begins to openly embrace deceitful practices, it reduces the moral purchase of other community members to commit to an alternative path [8].

The idea that all human beings are inconsolably intertwined is an idea and an ideal that often runs counter to the archetype of the autarchic individual—the individual who stands alone and resourceful against the world. It is the cry of the individual who seeks independence versus those who recognize that obligation to community simultaneously limits and liberates.

John Donne, in his memorable prose, No Man Is An Island, captures the sentiment that each person contributes to the existence of the other—that we are enhanced or diminished by the lives of our brothers and sisters.

No Man Is An Island

No man is an island,
Entire of itself.
Each is a piece of the continent,
A part of the main.
If a clod be washed away by the sea,
Europe is the less.
As well as if a promontory were.
As well as if a manor of thine own
Or of thine friend's were.
Each man's death diminishes me,
For I am involved in mankind.
Therefore, send not to know
For whom the bell tolls,
It tolls for thee.

Mediation XVII
Devotions upon Emergent Occasions
—John Donne

Learning, like so many other things, is relational. The ability to learn, as well as the process of learning, requires and is improved by participating in society and community. It is not only about the learner relating independently to the object of learning, but equally about interacting with other learners to interrogate, deepen and formalize the processes and outcomes of learning. In the words of professor emeritus George Hein (n.d.), distinguished professor from

Lesley College, "Learning is a social activity: our learning is intimately associated with our connection with other human beings, our teachers, our peers, our family as well as casual acquaintances, including the people before us or next to us at the exhibit. We are more likely to be successful in our efforts to educate if we recognize this principle rather than try to avoid it. Much of traditional education, as Dewey pointed out, is directed toward isolating the learner from all social interaction, and toward seeing education as a one-on-one relationship between the learner and the objective material to be learned. In contrast, progressive education (to continue to use Dewey's formulation) recognizes the social aspect of learning and uses conversation, interaction with others, and the application of knowledge as an integral aspect of learning."

Collaboration and achievement

In this context, if you want to be successful academically you must first recognize that this requires not only display of content mastery and other cognitive attributes, but also display of holistic development regarding interpersonal skills, communicative skills and other non-cognitive factors that are valued in professions and citizenship. This is the promise of collaborative activity to us. It offers a vital tool that we can use to multiply our individual academic achievement.

Barkley, Cross, and Major (2005), in what is regarded as the bible for collaborative learning, define collaborative learning as "two or more students laboring together and sharing the workload equitably as they progress toward intended learning outcomes." Two key features of collaborative learning can be identified from this definition: It is intentional and we must co-labor if meaningful learning is to occur (Barkley, et al., 2005).

Why it works

As collaborative learning emphasizes social interactions, it allows us to talk to each other in a natural social act. This dates to social constructivism, which proposes that we create meaning working together and this enriches us (Matthews, 1996 cited in Barkley et al., 2005).

Collaborative learning contributes to advancing academic achievement. Terenzini et al. (2001) provide evidence to show that the use of collaborative techniques for learning was statistically significant in promoting improved understanding and retention despite pre-course differences and variation in learning capabilities of college students. Explorations in cognition and neurology reveal that peer-to-peer interactions are effective techniques of active learning so that student erudition and retention are maximized.

Chickering and Gamson (1991), cited in Kaufman, Sutow and Dunn (1997), explain why collaboration works using the following analogy:

Learning is enhanced when it is more like a team effort than a solo race. Good learning, like good work, is collaborative and social, not competitive and isolated.

Working with others often increases involvement in learning. Sharing one's ideas and responding to others' reactions improves thinking and deepens understanding.

Benefits

Collaborative learning is more effective than traditional approaches to learning. Astin (1993), as cited in Kaufman, et al. (1997), reports that student-to-student interactions were the most influential factors affecting the largest number of general education outcomes. Terenzini et al. (2001) endorses these findings and suggests that collaborative approaches to learning are more effective than traditional approaches because they cater for differences in students' levels of preparation and learning styles. They conclude that active learning, via collaboration, produces greater gains in academic content and skills (as cited in Kaufman, et al., 1997).

A possible explanation for the improved academic performance experienced by students engaging in collaboration may be that peer group interaction offers more motivation to students to become more active participants in the learning process (Barkley, et al., 2005). You gain independence and assume responsibility for the success of the group. This improves your satisfaction and causes you to learn more. Consider the case of reciprocal teaching among students, a form of collaborative learning that is proven to advance achievement (Curtis & Lawson, 2001).

In collaborative discourse the cognitive load of the learning task is shared, there is greater on-task engagement and greater understanding (Curtis & Lawson, 2001). Thus, you are empowered by the approach and work hard to accomplish the group's goal.

Modern cognitive theory advocates that learners must be *actively engaged* in learning as we actually "build" our own understanding by actively constructing mental models or schemas that connect and organize information (Curtis & Lawson, 2001). Applied to collaborative learning, Curtis &

Lawson (2001) explains that students in groups have diverse backgrounds that overlap enough to form a common base for communication.

Thus, through this communication, all students are exposed to the concepts and understandings of each other that are within their capacity to grasp, but not yet personally learned. Thus, students utilizing collaborative learning techniques have quantifiably better reasoning and communication skills than students who do not. Empirical studies also indicate higher levels of achievement and greater retention with cooperative learning as opposed to individualist learning (Miller & Peterson, 2004). From the perspective of noted Russian educational psychologist Lev Vygotsky—who advocates social interaction as a necessary precursor of cognitive development—collaboration would allow the scaffolding of thinking, and quick feedback to the learner (Curtis & Lawson, 2001).

Collaboration develops the interpersonal and social skills of the learner. Behaviors such as providing and receiving aid, exchanging resources and information, challenging and motivating each other, and reflecting on progress are key elements of positive social interaction provided by collaborative activities (Curtis & Lawson, 2001). Students exposed to these report feelings of greater self-esteem and empowerment that in the traditional competitive classroom, particularly when the task is more complex and involves greater problem solving and creativity. This improves students' communication skills and their ability to deal with disagreements and conflict, valued traits in the world of employment. Thus, approaching tasks collaboratively better prepares you for participatory work as part of society (Fcichtner & Davis, 1991, cited in Baker & Clark, 2010)

Slavin (1990) identifies another major benefit of collaboration as a means for developing intercultural learning through collaboration with culturally diverse groups. This is particularly important when transitioning from secondary school to university life where student diversity is greater (Dalziel & Peat, 1998). The literature shows that students who are involved in collaborative learning had fewer problems 'fitting in' with university life, learned more about different cultures and were more tolerant of others. They were less likely to drop out of tertiary studies and were more academically motivated (Dalziel & Peat, 1998). These students had very positive attitudes toward each other and toward themselves.

The collaborative learning approach emerged as a means to nullify the overemphasis of competition in education. Research has consistently shown that collaborative learning approaches produces outcomes that are superior to those obtained through traditional competitive pedagogies. Today the mantra is *collaborate not compete*. How then should you engage in collaboration?

Collaborating for best results: Recommendations

First, it is important that you move away from competitive thinking: listen and share. Everyone has a right to make a contribution. Instead of trying to dominate all communications see it as an opportunity to analyze, review, and deepen understanding of content. This will make remembering the material easier and promotes critical thinking.

Second, make the collaboration intentional. Advertise to students and to your friends your desire to collaborate and structure the time you spend collaborating. This involves assigning roles to members and selecting the best environment and time for collaboration. In being open to collaboration, try to welcome diversity, as this will provide alternative perspectives and experiences to your own.

Third, do the work and commit. It is pointless to attempt to collaborate if we are unprepared to exert any real effort to the exercise. We can liken this to the proverb of expecting to reap before we sow. This means that once you have made connections with a team, and the goals of the group are shared and accepted, you need to work toward them. There can be no success if members of the team do not make concerted efforts. So do your part.

Finally, collaborative activities afford opportunities to incorporate technology for learning that we can capitalize on in this tech-savvy age. Wikis, wireless handheld technology, and video chat software offer a more dynamic collaborative learning experience that is not limited by time and space. It means that collaboration does not have to be limited by geography—it can be with students across campuses or countries as well.

The goal of collaborative learning is to develop autonomous or independent, articulate thinkers, outcomes that are critical for student success. And these skills transfer beyond the classroom because skill in collaborating is essential for participating in a democratic society (Kagan, 1994).

References

Ariely, D. (2012). The (Honest)Truth About Dishonesty: How We Lie To Everyone—Including Ourselves. New York: HarperCollins.

Astin, A. (1993). What Matters in College: Four Critical Years Revisited. Jossey Bass, San Francisco.

Baker, T., & Clark, J. (2010). Cooperative learning–a double-edged sword: a cooperative learning model for use with diverse student groups. *Intercultural Education, 21*(3), 257-268.

Barkley, E. F., Cross, K. P., & Major, C. H. (2004). *Collaborative learning techniques: A handbook for college faculty.* Jossey-Bass.

Chickering, A. W., & Gamson, Z. F. (1991). Appendix A: Seven principles for good practice in undergraduate education. New directions for teaching and learning, (47), 63-69.

Curtis, D. D. & Lawson, M. J. (2001). Exploring collaborative online learning. *Journal of Asynchronous Learning Network,* 5(1), 21-34.

Dalziel, J. & Peat, M. (1998). Fostering collaborative learning during student transition to tertiary education: An evaluation of academic and social benefits. In *Improving Student Learning: Improving Students as Learners.* Edited by C. Rust, The Oxford Centre for Staff and Learning Development, Oxford Brookes University, Oxford, (272-283)

Fiechtner, S. B., and Davis, E. A. (1992). Why Some Groups Fail: A Survey of Students' Experiences with Learning Groups." In A. Goodsell, M. Maher, V. Tinto, and Associates (eds.), *Collaborative Learning: A Sourcebook for Higher Education.* University Park: National Center on Postsecondary Teaching, Learning, and Assessment, Pennsylvania State University.

Hein, G. (n.d.). *Constructivist Learning Theory.* Retrieved from http://www.education.miami.edu/blantonw/2800/XBLANTON/READINGS/conlearn.html

Kagan, S. (1994). *Cooperative Learning.* San Clemente, California: Kagan Publishing.

Kaufman, D., Sutow, E., & Dunn, K. (1997). Three approaches to cooperative learning in higher education. *Canadian Journal of Higher Education, 27*(2/3), 37-66.

Matthews, R. S. (1996). Collaborative learning: Creating knowledge with students. in R. J. Menges, M. Weimer & associates (Eds.). *Teaching on solid ground: Using scholarship to improve practice.* Jossey-Bass, San Francisco.

Peterson, S. E., & Miller, J. A. (2004). Comparing the quality of students' experiences during cooperative learning and large-group instruction. *The Journal of Educational Research, 97*(3), 123-134.

Slavin, R. E. (1990). Cooperative learning: Theory, research, and practice. New Jersey: Prentice Hall.

Terenzini, P. T., Cabrera, A. F., Colbeck, C. L., Parente, J. M., & Bjorklund, S. A. (2001). Collaborative learning vs. lecture/discussion: Students' reported learning gains. *Journal of Engineering Education-Washington, 90*(1), 123-130.

CHAPTER 9: LAW OF REST—IF WE ARE TO BE ACADEMICALLY DEEP, WE MUST SLEEP!

Sleep is the best meditation

—His Holiness the Dalai Lama

Sleeping is for Wimps?

One of my Skype contacts had as his status a few days ago, "so much work and no time for sleep". We live in a culture where sleep is regarded as an impediment to the culture of efficiency, productivity, and effectiveness. Nowhere is this more notoriously epitomized than in the quote attributed to the prodigious rapper 50 Cent, "Sleep: sleep is for those people who are broke. I don't sleep. I might miss the opportunity to make a dream become a reality" (Manikundalam, 2011). In the currency of disposable time, sleep is often viewed as of first-order disposability. This is especially true on so many college campuses, as 'street credit' is given to those who go the longest without sleep in order to get work done.

In the modern cinematic American adaptation of the British novel, Sherlock Holmes, for example, we find Dr. John Watson, played by Lucy Liu, dispensing a prescription of stay-awake squats to help Holmes maintain his wakefulness and forensic attention in the unraveling of child predator cases (Season 1, Episode 3: Child Predator). While natural remedies to keep sleep at bay abound, chemical solutions are also readily available: from caffeine to a range of energy stimulants.

Studies show that sacrificing sleep to produce more study time fuels a negative dynamic (Society for Research in Child Development, 2012). Indeed, sleep deprivation has a debilitating effect on cognition, and one's ability to perform at optimal capacity. Research has unearthed several pertinent findings in this discussion.

Academic Performance and Sleep Quality/Quantity

Across the academic plane, from primary through university schools, many students are chronically sleep deprived, experiencing poor quality sleep, which results in daytime sleepiness (Curcio, 2006). A student's ability to learn and to perform well academically is adversely affected when sleep quality or quantity are interrupted to the point of chronic daytime sleepiness. According to the National Sleep Foundation, 28% of US high school students reported falling asleep in school at least once per week because of not getting the recommended amount of sleep on a nightly basis of nine hours. Only 20% of teens reported that they get the recommended number of hours of sleep (Stage of Life, n.d.).

Research indicates that sleep loss' harmful effects on thinking and learning arises because of the vulnerability of the prefrontal cortex to sleep deprivation (Curcio, 2006).

American psychologist and sleep expert, David Dinges PhD states that if a person does not sleep after the initial signs of sleep deprivation (irritability, moodiness, disinhibition), they may begin to experience slow speech, apathy, flatter emotional responses, impaired memory, and impaired ability to be innovative or to multitask (American Psychological Association, n.d.).

Gomes et al. (2011) surveyed some 1654 full-time university students and found that in addition to previous academic achievement, class attendance, and night outings, "self-reported sleep quality and self-reported frequency of sufficient sleep were among the main predictors of academic performance." These findings are confirmed by Becker et al. (2008) who reviewed data provided by some 54,111 participants across 71 institutions pooled in the National College Health Assessment data. Their results showed that males and females who reported "good sleep" were more likely to perform academically better.

Sleep is like residual income, it works for us when we are not working. Put another way:

> During the day, each separate area of the brain temporarily absorbs information, similar to a holding tank. During sleep, the day's absorbed information is processed and relocated to permanent storage areas. And, each stage of sleep plays a different role in the processing of information. After a particularly grueling day of class—think mental exhaustion—kids need even longer sleep time so that the brain can properly process and store information. (Oxford Learning, 2007)

Snooze and Lose [9]

The body of research reviewed indicated that the following comprises some of the effects of sleep deprivation on the capacity to learn. They include:

- Poor declarative learning in students (i.e., unable to memorize facts);
- Poor procedural learning in students (i.e., reduced ability to learn a new skill through repeated practice and performance);
- Reduction in ability to think, remember, concentrate, learn, and understanding—and thus a deterioration in general academic performance;
- Significant reductions in performance and alertness. Losing one and a half hours of one night's of regular sleep time could lower daytime alertness by as much as 32% (Breus, n.d.).

- "Decreased alertness and excessive daytime sleepiness impair your memory and your cognitive ability—your ability to think and process information" (Breus, n.d.).
- "Increased sleep-onset latency—the time it takes to fall asleep once in bed—over the weekend was associated with worse academic performance" (American Academy of Sleep Science, 2009).
- "According to [Jennifer] Cousins, poor sleep and poor sleep habits are associated with substance use, emotional problems, cognitive problems and a general decline in daily functioning. Sleep education may be a preventative tool to help increase awareness of the importance of sleep and of the negative consequences of poor sleep (American Academy of Sleep Science, 2009); and,
- Lower levels of motivation, difficulty concentrating in class; and difficulty staying awake in class (Dallas, 2011).

Sleep Quality

Gray and Watson (2002) reveal in their research that sleep quality affects greater well-being and improved psychological functioning. They also found that those who exhibited the personality trait of Conscientiousness [10]—regarded as a facet of academic striving—maintained earlier schedules, rising and sleeping earlier. Sleep quality, less awakenings, and increased sleep efficiency have also been shown to correlate strongly with improved math scores (American Academy of Sleep Science, 2009). Jennifer Cousins confirms the same in a research of 592 students aged 12 to 19 years; those who were able to fall asleep more quickly as soon as they went to bed, performed academically better than the rest (Lawrence, 2012).

Action plan: A good night's sleep (American Psychological Association, n.d.).

- Get regular exercise.
- Keep a regular sleep/wake schedule.
- Don't drink or eat caffeine four to six hours before bed and minimize daytime consumption of caffeine.
- Don't smoke, especially near bedtime or if you awake in the night.
- Avoid alcohol and heavy meals before sleep.
- Minimize noise, light and excessive hot and cold temperatures where you sleep.

- Give yourself an extra hour before bed to relax and unwind and time to write down worries and plans for the following day.
- Attempt to go to bed earlier every night for certain period; this will ensure that you're getting enough sleep.
- If unable to sleep, get out of bed and try reading for twenty minutes before returning to bed.
- Avoid snoozing, as this does not lead to a restful sleep: Try to wake up without an alarm clock.
- Maintain a consistent study schedule across days so that it is not necessary to give up sleep in order to study (Science Daily, 2012).
- Use school time as efficiently as possible and sacrifice time spent on other less essential activities, in order to not have to give up sleeping time (Science Daily, 2012).
- Choose classes that start later in the morning where possible—this will improve sleep duration, reduce daytime sleepiness, and reduce likelihood of missing

class. This requires self-discipline as students who start classes late tend to increase likelihood of alcohol abuse and thus negatively affect academic performance (Onyper et al., 2012).

- Avoid watching television in bed, as this encourages poor sleep habits/patterns.
- Avoid doing homework immediately before (or in) bed, and avoid computer use before bed.
- If napping during the day, keep to short power naps of 10-45 minutes. Research shows that napping 10-45 minutes (before entering REM sleep) can increase performance.
- Go to bed only when sleepy, and get out of bed when unable to sleep (American Psychological Association, n.d.).

References

American Academy of Sleep Medicine (2009, June 15). Better Sleep Is Associated With Improved Academic Success. *Science Daily*.

American Psychological Association (n.d.). *Importance of sleep.* Retrieved from http://www.apa.org/topics/sleep/why.aspx.

Becker, C. M., Adams, T., Orr, C., & Quilter, L. (2008). Correlates of Quality Sleep and Academic Performance. *Health Educator*, *40*(2), 82-89.

Breus, M. (n.d.) Sleep Habits: More Important Than You Think. *MyWebMD.* Retrieved from http://www.webmd.com/sleep-disorders/features/important-sleep-habits

Bronson, P (2007, October 7). Snooze or Lose. *New York.* Retrieved from http://nymag.com/news/features/38951/

Cari Gillen-O'Neel, Virginia W. Huynh, Andrew J. Fuligni. (2012). To Study or to Sleep? The Academic Costs of Extra Studying at the Expense of Sleep. *Child Development.* doi: 10.1111/j.1467-8624.2012.01834.x

Curcio, G., Ferrara, M., & De Gennaro, L. (2006). Sleep loss, learning capacity and academic performance. *Sleep medicine reviews*, *10*(5), 323.

Dallas, M (2011, September 19). Lack of Sleep Hurts Kids' Academic Performance: Study. *Health.* Retrieved from http://news.health.com/2011/09/19/lack-of-sleep-hurts-kids-academic-performance-study/

Gomes, A. A., Tavares, J., & de Azevedo, M. H. P. (2011). Sleep and Academic Performance in Undergraduates: A Multi-measure, Multi-predictor Approach. *Chronobiology International*, *28*(9), 786-801.

Gray, E. K., & Watson, D. (2002). General and specific traits of personality and their relation to sleep and academic performance. *Journal of Personality, 70*(2), 177-206.

Lawrence, J (2012, October 17). More Sleep Improves Mood, Academic Outcomes, Study Finds. *Education News.* Retrieved from http://www.educationnews.org/parenting/more-sleep-improves-mood-academic-outcomes-study-finds/

Manikundalam, A. (2011, October 19). *When do you sleep? 50 I don't sleep.* Retrieved from http://arunmanikundalam.wordpress.com/2011/10/19/when-do-you-sleep-50-i-dont-sleep-i-might-miss-the-opportunity-to-make-a-dream-become-a-reality-50-cent/

Onyper, S., Thacher, P, Gilbert, J, & Gradess, S. (2012). Class Start Times, Sleep, and Academic Performance in College: A Path Analysis.*Chronobiology international, 29*(3), 318-335.

Oxford Learning (2007, October 11). *Sleep Habits and Academic Performance.* Retrieved from http://www.oxfordlearning.com/letstalk/2007/10/11/sleep-habits/

Society for Research in Child Development (2012, August 21). Sacrificing sleep to study can lead to academic problems. *Science Daily*.

Stage of Life (n.d.). Statistics on high school students and teenagers. Retrieved from http://www.stageoflife.com/StageHighSchool/OtherResources/Statistics_on_High_School_Students_and_Teenagers.aspx

CHAPTER 10: LIVE RIGHT TO LEARN RIGHT—HEALTHY CHOICES AND MINDFULNESS

You cannot educate a child who is not healthy and you cannot keep a child healthy who is not educated.
　　—Dr. Joycelyn Elders, former US Surgeon General

Mens sana in corpore sano -- A sound mind in a sound body

The Roman poet Juvenal, in response to the question about what is desirable in life, penned his answer in satire. The English translation of the original Latin verses is reproduced below:

You should pray for a sound mind in a sound body.

Ask for a stout heart that has no fear of death,

and deems length of days the least of Nature's gifts

that can endure any kind of toil,

that knows neither wrath nor desire and thinks

the woes and hard labors of Hercules better than

the loves and banquets and downy cushions

of Sardanapalus [11].

What I commend to you, you can give to yourself;

For assuredly, the only road to a life of peace lies in that of virtue.

–Roman poet Juvenal (10.356-64)

His poem praises the gift of a virtuous life, as a gift within the range of humanity's grasp. Juvenal privileges this pursuit as more worthy of humanity's aspirations than the singular longing for a long life. For Juvenal, culturing a heart that is not quickly or easily moved by emotional upsets, and that does not sway in the face of challenge and contest, will lead to peace through virtue. For Juvenal, peace is the end of a one-way street called virtue.

The wisdom of seeking a sound mind to cohabit a sound body pre-dates the first-century AD. Juvenal, in the fifth-century BC, figure of the pre-Socratic Greek philosopher Thales of Miletus—who is the starting point of Western Philosophy, if we cede to the judgment of

Bertrand Russell (1945). It is a timeless counsel, adopted by athletes, leaders, politicians, educators, and philosophers. It is the motto of a range of athletic, academic, and military institutions. John Locke, 17th century English philosopher and physician, defended the interconnectedness of education and physical wellness. He stated the following:

A SOUND mind in a sound body, is a short, but full description of a happy state in this world. He that has these two, has little more to wish for; and he that wants either of them, will be but little the better for anything else. Men's happiness or misery is most part of their own making. He, whose mind directs not wisely, will never take the right way; and he, whose body is crazy and feeble, will never be able to advance in it. (The Harvard Classics, 1909-14)

Academic Performance and Healthy Living: The Research

Alcohol, Tobacco, and Drug Use

Healthy living intersects with many domains of our life: our physicality; our sexuality; our diet; and our socializing. Lifestyles that abuse, misuse, or neglect the body negatively affect the body's ability to deliver optimal cognitive performances.

One of the forms of this abuse is substance and alcohol abuse (CADCA, 2010). Research indicates that substance use precipitates academic difficulties including lower grades, absenteeism, and high dropout rates (Dewey, 1999). Early initiation into substance use has long-term adverse effects on life outcomes, with the research indicating that the onset of violent and delinquent behavior, poor physical health, and mental health problems extending into adolescence and early adulthood (Griffin, 2003).

The use of illicit drugs, alcohol, and tobacco can negatively affect a student's thinking ability, impairing concentration and making learning difficult. The frequent use and abuse of tobacco, alcohol, and illicit drugs is associated with lower grade point averages (Dewey, 1999; Johnston, 1998). According to the 2009 National Youth Risk Behavior Survey (YRBS), there is a negative association between alcohol and drug use, and academic achievement.

Alcohol use and abuse may affect memory and the ability to produce work of an acceptable standard of quality (Brown et al., 2000). Drinking on college campuses has been associated with fighting, acquaintance rape, unprotected sex, with deleterious effects on college campuses (The Higher Education Center, 2003). According to the National Institute on Alcohol Abuse and Alcoholism Task Force on College Drinking, a quarter of college students admit that alcohol use has caused them to achieve lower grades, perform poorly in tests and on papers, miss class, and fall behind (The Higher Education Center, 2003). A national survey of 94,000 students found that students with an A average generally consumed about 4 drinks per week, B students 6 drinks, C students 8 drinks, and D or F students roughly 10 drinks per week (Pressley, 1999).

Diet and Exercise

The research is indeed non-contentious on the matter: there is a strong positive correlation between a healthy diet, or diet quality, and academic performance (Centers for Disease Control and Prevention, 2011; Basch, 2011). Alternately, those with poor nutrition have lower academic results, as indicated by tests on vocabulary, reading comprehension, arithmetic, and general knowledge (Brown et al., 1996). However, what do we mean by healthy eating or dietary habits? Characteristically, healthy eating habits win on two components: adequacy and variety.

A healthy diet includes a range of food types, sufficient intake of minerals and vitamins, protein and fiber, adequate vegetables and fruits, and moderate consumption of fat (Alberta Health Services, n.d.). This means that a person is eating a good variety of foods in the course of the day; and the food is appropriate as per gender, age, activity level, and life cycle. Unhealthy or less healthy foods consist of those that have a higher concentration of sugar or fat and lower amounts of vitamins or minerals. These are of poorer nutritional value, and diet quality, and may lead to weight gain over time. Some examples of these are: potato chips, French fries, hamburgers, hotdogs, and sweetened beverages (Alberta Health Services, n.d.).

According to data from the 2009 National Youth Risk Behavior Survey, students who were achieving academically higher outcomes were less likely to have participated in any of the following behaviors: watching television for at least three hours per day on an average school day; playing video or computer games, or using the computers for at least three hours per day on non-school work activity; drinking a can, bottle, or glass of soda or pop at least once per day (for the week before the survey); not eating for twenty-four hours or more (for weight loss or to prevent weight gain, over the thirty-day period before the survey); being physically active for at least an hour on less than five of the seven days prior to the survey (CDC, n.d.).

Eating, as in so many other activities of life, is about getting the right balance. The consumption of too much food, or of food that is less healthy, compounded with little physical activity, can produce weight gain. Contrarily, insufficient consumption of food can adversely affect a person's physical development, behavior for learning, and ability to learn. Indeed, malnutrition and hunger negatively affect intelligence and academic performance. Temporary hunger reduces attention, interest, and learning. That's why a healthy breakfast is an important start to the day (Hodgkin, n.d.).

By eating healthy, research indicates that students are able to perform better on standardized tests, and achieve higher grade point averages. Conversely, a poor diet is associated with lower achievement in core language and math courses (Alberta Health Services, n.d.). Overweight students, especially girls, tend to have diminished academic accomplishments, and have greater challenges in math and reading (Alberta Health Services, n.d.).

The mechanics

A healthy diet contains key nutrients that support optimal cognitive functioning. Effective studying requires a brain to be alert and retentive—and this is provided for by an adequately nutritious diet. What we eat and drink provides energy and nutrition to the body's organs and its systems. Such energy and nutrition are necessary for the body to function optimally and to repair itself. If a student does not have energy for cognition, he or she will feel less connected to his or her studies, and therefore less inclined to attend classes, further hindering academic progress (Basch, 2011)

Carbohydrates, protein, and fats are the sources of the body's energy. Carbohydrates are broken down into glucose, the only energy-form that the brain can absorb (Magistretti et al., n.d.). The breakdown of starches and sugars, the constituent elements of carbohydrates, requires other nutrients such as vitamins and minerals. Protein is also a critical resource for nourishing the brain as it helps to repair cells, and maintain body function. Finally, the brain and central nervous system requires fat to support the functioning of the myelin sheath, which is the fatty layer that encases the nerves. The sheath, 70% fat and 30% protein, helps nerves to transmit their signals, and if damaged, can affect memory (Ortega, n.d.; The Franklin Institute, n.d.). Nutrition also affects neurotransmitters, which play an important role in communicating messages between the body and the brain (Ross, 2010, p. 3).

If a diet lacks iron, and to the extent that it induces anemia, then it may result in poor cognition, narrow attention span, difficulty in concentrating, tiredness, and lower standardized math, vocabulary, and reading scores (Hodgkin, n.d.). Those following a vegetarian or vegan diet and teenage girls would need to supplement their diet to avoid iron deficiency because of the higher need for iron. A similar adverse effect on cognitive functioning can arise if there is insufficient supply or availability of a safe and nutrient-rich diet.

Recommendation

First, choose your friends carefully. Students who had peers who avoided substance abuse performed better on assessments in reading and mathematics (CADCA, 2010; Bence et al., 2000). Peers' approval of one's risky behaviors can negatively influence one's lifestyle choices, whereas parents' disapproval of risky behaviors is a positive influence (He et al., 2004).

Second, starting the day right with a healthy breakfast can significantly affect academic outcomes. Research indicates that a healthy breakfast improves short-term cognition, school attendance, mood, psychosocial function, scores on mathematics tests, scores on memory and creativity tests, and physical endurance (Rampersaud et al., 2005; Alberta Health Services, n.d). According to the Mayo Clinic, a healthy breakfast improves concentration, enables better problem-solving skills, improves hand-eye coordination, fosters alertness, and reduces school absenteeism (Mayo Clinic n.d.). In general, it promotes physical well-being, which sponsors improved academic outcomes.

What constitutes a healthy breakfast? The Mayo Clinic does not leave us without expert guidance on this matter:

- Whole grains: whole-grain rolls, bagels, hot or cold whole grain cereals, low-fat bran muffins, crackers, or Melba toast.
- Low-fat protein: peanut butter, lean meat, poultry or fish, or hardboiled eggs.
- Low-fat dairy: skim milk, low-fat yogurt, and low-fat

cheeses, such as cottage and natural cheeses.

- Fruits and vegetables: fresh or frozen fruits and vegetables, 100% juice beverages without added sugar, or fruit and vegetable smoothies. Choose the low-sodium versions of beverages.

Together, these core groups provide complex carbohydrates, fiber, protein and a small amount of fat—a combination that packs big health benefits and that also can leave you feeling full for hours. Choose one or two options from each category to round out a healthy breakfast (Mayo Clinic, n.d.).

Third, strengthen the immune system by including Vitamin A and zinc in your diet. Vitamin A can be found in orange and green vegetables; while zinc can be found in fortified grains, animal foods, and legumes. A strong immune system helps to fight infections, and helps to maintain the body's health (Stein, 2010).

Ryan Palmer

Summary of Dietary Guidelines

1. Consume a variety of nutrient-dense foods and beverages.

2. Maintain body weight in a healthy range.

3. Engage in regular physical activity.

4. Choose a variety of fruits and vegetables every day.

5. Consume three or more ounces of whole grains daily.

6. Consume three cups per day of fat-free or low-fat milk products.

7. Keep total fat intake between 20% and 35% of calories; limit trans-fat and cholesterol.

8. Choose and prepare foods and beverages with little added sugar.

9. Consume less than 2300mg of sodium per day.

10. Clean your hands, food contact surfaces, and fruits and vegetables.

From US Department of Agriculture and US Department of Health and Human Services, Nutrition and Your Health: Dietary Guidelines for Americans (Washington, DC: 2005).

13 Keys To Genius

www.mypyramid.gov

References

Alberta Health Services (n.d.). *Healthy Eating and School Performance: An Evidence summary*. Retrieved from http://www.albertahealthservices.ca/SchoolsTeachers/if-sch-nfs-evidence-brief-school-performance.pdf

Basch, C. E. (2011). Healthier students are better learners: A missing link in school reforms to close the achievement gap. *Journal of School Health, 81*(10), 593-598.

Bence, M. Brandon, R., Lee, I., & Tran, H. University of Washington. (2000). *Impact of peer substance use on middle school performance in Washington: Summary*. Washington Kids Count/University of WA: Seattle, WA. Available: http://wwww.hspc.org/wkc/special/pdf/peer_sub_091200.pdf.

Borzack (2010-10-22). How A Healthy Lifestyle Affects College Student's Academic Performance. *Healthy lifestyle*. Retrieved from http://healthy-lifestyle.most-effective-solution.com/2010/10/22/how-a-healthy-lifestyle-affects-college-students-academic-performance/

Brown, L. & Pollitt, E. (1996). Malnutrition, Poverty and Intellectual Development. *Scientific American, 274*(2), 38-43.

Brown, S. A., Tapert, S. F., Granholm, E., et al. (2000). Neurocognitive functioning of adolescents: Effects of protracted alcohol use. *Alcoholism: Clinical and experimental research, 24*(2).

CADCA (2010). The Forgotten Link: Drug and Alcohol Use and Academic Achievement. Retrieved from http://www.cadca.org/policyadvocacy/priorities/safe-and-drug-free-schools-and-communities-program/Toolkit.

CDC (n.d.). Physical Inactivity and Unhealthy Dietary Behaviors and Academic Achievement. Retrieved from http://www.cdc.gov/healthyyouth/health_and_academics/pdf/physical_inactivity_unhealthy_weight.pdf

Centers For Disease Control and Prevention. (2011m November 4). *Health & Academics*. Retrieved from http://www.cdc.gov/HealthyYouth/health_and_academics/.

Dewey, J. D. (1999). Reviewing the relationship between school factors and substance use for elementary, middle and high school students. *Journal of Primary Prevention, 19*(3), 177-225. http://www.med.cornell.edu/ipr/PDF/Griffin-et-al-2003-PM.pdf

The Franklin Institute (n.d.). The Human Brain. Retrieved from http://www.fi.edu/learn/brain/fats.html

Greenblatt, J. C. (2000). *Patterns of alcohol use among adolescents and associations with emotional and behavioral problems.* Rockville, MD: Substance Abuse and Mental Health Services and Administration, Office of Applied Studies.

Griffin, K. W., Botvin, G. J., Nichols, T. R., & Doyle, M. M. (2003). Effectiveness of a universal drug abuse prevention approach for youth at high risk for substance use initiation. *Preventive Medicine, 36*(1), 1-7.

He, K., Kramer, E., Houser, R. F., Chomitz, V. R., & Hacker, K. A. (2004). Defining and understanding healthy lifestyles choices for adolescents. *Journal of Adolescent Health, 35*(1), 26-33.

The Higher Education Center (2003). *College Academic Performance and Alcohol and Other Drug Use.* Retrieved from http://www.higheredcenter.org/files/product/fact_sheet2.pdf

Hodgkin, G. (n.d.). Nutrition and academic achievement: Are they related? *Dialogue* Retrieved from http://dialogue.adventist.org/articles/20_1_hodgkin_e.htm

Johnston, L. D., O'Malley, P. M., & Bachman, J. G. (1998). *National survey results on drug use from the Monitoring the Future study, 1975-1999, Volume I: Secondary school students.* Rockville, MD: U.S. Department of Health and Human Services. Public Health Services, National Institutes of Health, National Institute on Drug Abuse.

Locke, J. (1632-1704). Some Thoughts Concerning Education. *The Harvard Classics.* 1909-1914.

Mayo Clinic (n.d.) *Nutrition and Healthy Eating.* Retrieved from http://www.mayoclinic.com/health/food-and-nutrition/NU00197

Ortega, B. (n.d.). How to Repair the Myelin Sheath with Food. *eHow Health.* Retrieved from http://www.ehow.com/how_7894361_repair-myelin-sheath-food.html

Magistretti, P. J., Pellerin, L., & Martin, J.-L. (). Brain Energy Metabolism. An Integrated Cellular Perspective. Book Chapter from *Psychopharmacology—4th Generation of Progress*, Floyd E. Bloom, MD & David J. Kupfer, MD.

Presley C. A., Leichliter J. S., Meilman, P. W. (1999). Alcohol and Drugs on American College Campuses: Finding from 1995, 1996, and 1997. *A Report to College Presidents.* Carbondale, IL: Southern Illinois University.

Rampersaud G., Pereira M., Girard B., Adams J., Metzel J. (2005). Breakfast habits, nutritional status, body weight and academic performance in children and adolescents. *Journal of American Dietary Association*, 105, 743-760.

Ross, A. (2010). *Nutrition and Its Effect On Academic Performance: How Can Our Schools Improve?* (Masters Thesis). Retrieved from http://www.nmu.edu/sites/DrupalEducation/files/UserFiles/Files/Pre-Drupal/SiteSections/Students/GradPapers/Projects/Ross_Amy_MP.pdf

Russell, B. (1945). *The History of Western Philosophy.* New York, NY: Simon and Schuster.

Singleton, R. A., & Wolfson, A. R. (2009). Alcohol consumption, sleep, and academic performance among college students. *Journal of studies on alcohol and drugs, 70*(3), 355.

Stein, N. (2010, September 27). *Diet and Academic Performance.* Retrieved from Livestrong.com http://www.livestrong.com/article/245090-diet-academic-performance/

WSU ADCAPS (n.d.) *Sleep and Academic Performance.* Retrieved from http://adcaps.wsu.edu/factoids/sleep-academic-performance/

Ryan Palmer

Chapter 11: The Law of Exercise

The Greeks understood that mind and body must develop in harmonious proportions to produce a creative intelligence. And so did the most brilliant intelligence of our earliest days—Thomas Jefferson—when he said, not less than two hours a day should be devoted to exercise. If the man who wrote the Declaration of Independence, was Secretary of State, and twice President, could give it two hours, our children can give it ten or fifteen minutes.

—John F Kennedy, Address to the National Football Foundation, 5 Dec 1961

Challenging the Times

The dumb jock (athlete) is a stereotype that has cemented itself in the cultural psyche or Zeitgeist, that is, spirit of our time. He goes by a variety of names including meathead and muscle brain. His pedigree lies in his physical or sporting prowess, at the expense of his cognitive development. The stereotypical jock is, therefore, usually unenlightened and unintelligent, although physically or socially advantaged. He excels at football or basketball, and may be from a wealthy family, and so the dumb jock stereotype overlaps with the preppie stereotype. Moose Mason, from the Archie cartoons, probably ranks as one of the well-known faces of the dumb jock—a muscular star-athlete who is dyslexic and poor at his studies [12].

Patrick Lee Trammel was anything but stereotypical. Born in Scottsboro, Alabama in 1940 to a local physician, Dr. Edward Lee Trammell, he showed himself as proficient at both athletics and academics. He was the starting quarterback in varsity football for Scottsboro High School. During his four-year high school career, he earned All-County, All-State, All-Southern, and All-American honors. Recruited by Paul 'Bear' Bryant to the University of Alabama, he would play for the Crimson Tide from 1958 to 1961. In 1959, Trammell led Alabama in total offense. In 1960, he led in total scoring, and Alabama was named SEC champion.

The year 1961 would prove to be the fruition of the promise held by the previous seasons: Trammell would lead the team to a perfect season, 11-0-0; and, ultimately gather a NCAA Championship, the first in sixteen years for Alabama. He would receive national recognition on television as, together with Coach Bryant, he would accept the MacArthur Trophy from President John Kennedy, at the National Football Foundation's reception held at the Grand Ballroom at the Waldorf-Astoria in New York, on December 5, 1961. However, Trammel's story was cut short by testicular cancer, dying at the age of 28, shortly after earning his M.D. degree.

Sound body for a sound mind

Athleticism and academic skill need not cohabit different spheres. Indeed, if we take a systems-approach to understanding the functioning of the body, we notice that the brain and the body are inseparably intertwined—each affecting the other. As we know, the body is a system and is made of various organs and muscles. Just like the other muscles in our body, our brain has its functions. We exercise to stimulate the growth of muscle cells; in the same way, we use brain fitness to increase neural connections in our brains. According to a study done by the Department of Exercise Science at the University of Georgia (Physical Exercise for Brain Health, 2012), briefly exercising for twenty minutes facilitates information processing and memory functions. Brain fitness, together with physical exercise, increases our ability to function cognitively, taking into consideration the type of physical exercise and the time of the exercise.

Exercise that involves both physical and mental demands, such as ballroom dancing, has a larger effect on cognitive functions as opposed to just exercise or mental tasks alone. Therefore, exercises that involve coordination, rhythm, and strategy give the best brain workouts. Exercise pumps oxygen to the brain and helps in releasing various hormones, which are necessary for the growth of brain cells. Research at UCLA (Physical Exercise for Brain Health, 2012) found that exercise increases growth factors in the brain, thus making it easier for brain to grow new neuronal connections. Behavior has a lot to do with learning and achievement, and exercise helps in this regard as well. A study from Stockholm (Physical Exercise for Brain Health, 2012) showed that the antidepressant effect of running was also associated with more cell growth in the hippocampus, an area of the brain responsible for learning and memory.

Exercise and academic achievement

According to research done by the University of Illinois (Castelli et al., 2007) a positive link was found between physical activity, attention, and academic achievement in children. In the research, it was noted that after doing sessions of exercise before academic classes, they were able to pay attention and performed better. It also showed that the older children should have more physical activity than younger children should.

According to Charles Hillman and Darla Castelli (2007), professors of kinesiology and community health, physical activity may increase students' cognitive control—or ability to pay attention—and also result in better performance on academic achievement tests. They found that students who engaged in physical activity, such as walking on a treadmill, were more alert when tested as opposed to those sitting and resting before similar tests. The students were tested in reading, math, and spelling. After doing sessions of exercise the students did a lot better, especially at reading comprehension.

Research done by the California Department of Education (2001) showed that conditions that improve general health, such as exercise, promote both a healthy body and an improved intellectual capacity. The study found that students who did better on achievement tests were also more physically fit than their peers who did not do well. This study compared students' Fitnessgram [13] scores with their reading and math scores on the Stanford Achievement Test [14]. The test was done for students from grades five, seven, and nine. The author Jim Grissom

(2004) stated that there is a positive relationship between overall fitness and academic achievement.

He noted, "students who get regular physical education and exercise are better able to concentrate in the classroom. Exercise can help reduce asthma symptoms, a major cause for student absenteeism, especially in low-income areas. Regular exercise can alleviate stress, anxiety, and depression—problems that can affect school performance—and can even boost self-esteem." Taras (2005) a member of the American Academy of Pediatrics Task Force on Obesity, reported strong evidence that physical activity promotes student concentration and focus, for the short term at least.

A group of ADHD students was assessed over a six-week period by Mike Wendt, a superintendent of Wilson Central School District in Wilson N.Y., along with the University of Buffalo (Vail, 2006). They said, "We saw a dramatic behavior change at the end of six weeks." Because of that study, the district applied for and won a federal

Physical Education Program (PEP) grant for $250,000 to build fitness centers at its schools. These centers were used for, and not limited to, exercise among other things for the students at risk. It was also noted that certain types of exercises could enhance focus and relieve stress. Lessons could be perfectly planned and executed but that does not guarantee that the students will learn. Florida's Ellen Smith (Vail, 2006) states, "if they are uptight and their brain, mind, and body are not ready to learn, it will be a wasted effort." Therefore, exercise can be a way of helping them to relax and focus.

Dwyer et al. (2001) did similar studies with students in Australia. The students were given indoor and outdoor tests. They were tested on a five-point scale, which includes excellent, above average, average, below average and poor ratings. After reviewing the results Dwyer et al. (2001) noted "consistently across age and sex groups, the [academic] ratings were significantly correlated with questionnaire measures of physical activity and with performance on the 1.6 kilometer run, sit-ups, and push-ups challenges, fifty-meter sprint, and standing long jump". This contradicts the myth that students normally good at sports are not academically sound. Linder (1999) did similar studies relates to students in Hong Kong and found that there was a positive relationship between physical activity and perceived academic performance.

Exercises: How they work and which one works for you

There are several reasons hypothesized about why exercise permits such an effect on cognition, and in turn on academic performance. First, it increases blood flow and oxygen flow to the brain. Second, it reduces stress level and improves mood by increasing the levels of norepinephrine and endorphins. Third, increased growth factors in the brain help to create new nerve cells and to support synaptic plasticity (Safe Routes to School, n.d.).

According to research from the University of North Texas, cardio-respiratory fitness registered as the most significant factor in the academic performance of middle school students, especially as it relates to math and reading (Srikanth et al., n.d.). Having a healthy heart and lungs can, therefore, help to improve verbal and quantitative reasoning. In research done by Hillman et al. (2005), they explored the effects of the aerobics. They noted that increased physical activity was related to eight measurement categories. Their results were favorable on the levels of the eight measurement categories except memory.

Walking was another exercise that was tested to see how it relates to students' cognitive functions. Hillman et al. (2005) experimented with twenty students and tested their brain reaction after resting, and after walking, both activities for twenty minutes. It showed that more areas of the brain became active after walking, as opposed to after resting. This demonstrates that walking helps your brain to function in a lot more areas than just relaxing.

Mitchell (1997) researched and found that there is a relationship between the rhythmic competency of first graders and their academic performance. Considering that exercise involves some form of coordination, exercise helps to condition the brain to seek patterns and similarities, thus making it amenable to subjects such as mathematics and reading.

Exercise enhances students' energy levels and thus increases their self-esteem and their behavior, which in turn will boost academic performance. In addition, exercise improves health thus giving students greater opportunity to be present at school, and having greater opportunity to learn. Overall, exercise increases flexibility, strength, endurance, body composition, and especially discipline, which if transferred to academics will produce higher rates of achievement.

Exercise and you

Exercise can help to improve brain activity and thus boost one's academic performance. Instead of sitting for extended periods talking to friends and waiting for a lecture, walk around while you talk. This will help your energy level to increase and cause more aspects of the brain to become active.

Exercise pumps oxygen to the brain, which in turn helps with the growth of brain cells. Exercise such as aerobics increases P3 latency—a brain potential that is related to orienting and involuntary shifts in changes in the environment. P3 latency has been associated with gifted children and thus if this is amplified normally because of aerobics then it could be of benefit to all children. P3 latency enables students to adapt easily to changes or to a variety of concepts.

As we age, the brain retains the capacity to grow new neurons. Severe mental decline is usually caused by disease, whereas most age-related losses in memory or motor skills simply result from inactivity, and a lack of mental exercise and stimulation. Therefore, instead of sitting around studying for a test get up, walk in a rhythm, jog, or engage in dancing, such as ballroom dancing, which places demands on not only the physical but also the mental.

Timing, coordination, and rhythm help to enhance your brain functions, thus helping to make sense of the information being studied, and aiding in memory. Learning things in patterns can help in subjects such as mathematics, a subject proven to be a challenge to many students. Additionally, on large college campuses instead of driving, one can exercise before the next class by walking or jogging if possible.

Instead of sleeping at various hours of the day, before a test, take a walk or jog to get the body active and to cause more neurons to be created in the brain, thus enhancing one's cognitive capabilities, making it easier to memorize and thus perform better. Many students start on a high and soon lose the zeal they had. They become inactive, and inactivity has been associated with loss of neurons. Vanaman (2011), commenting on a study done in March 2007 in the Proceedings of the National Academy of Sciences, stated that neurogenesis in some parts of the brain can be easily induced with exercise.

Recommendations and Actionable Strategies

- Research indicates that the best time to exercise is when the body's temperature is at its highest, improving our body's readiness for exercise. By experimenting with different exercise times during the day over a period of weeks, we can determine which time is best for us and which time will be sustainable, given daily and weekly routines (Gardner, 2012).
- Schedule exercise for the same time each day, and after eating, especially after a large meal, is best (Gardner, 2012).

- Most people who report a consistent exercise regime do so in the morning where there are minimum distractions and interruptions. This can provide increased energy levels, increased metabolism, and mental alertness for the day ahead (Gardner, 2012).
- Exercise for at least twenty minutes doing activities such as walking, jogging, or aerobics increases memory functions and information processing.
- Ballroom dancing is a good way of getting more out of exercise time.
- Engaging in twenty minutes of exercise for five days can increase stability and focus.
- Exercise needs to be planned and structured, as this will reduce injuries or strains on various parts of the body.
- With exercise comes proper rest as well. Without proper rest one could have circulation problems or as serious as a chance of stroke.

- Exercise should be controlled by each body's inherent limitations. While one set of joints and muscles may have the tolerance to withstand multiple marathons, another body may be damaged by twenty minutes of light jogging.
- Take a twenty minute walk before your tests or exams—aerobic exercise produces specific growth factors and proteins that stimulate the brain
- Twenty minutes of playing sports-style video games at a similar intensity is not a substitute for actual physical activity and does not carry the cognitive effects of physical aerobic exercise (Santos, 2011).
- Exercising before class can be beneficial to improving test scores and course grade.
- Limit daily television, video games, and computer time as daily consumption of the same for non-academic purposes has been shown to negate the benefits of

exercising, while encouraging emotional and behavioral difficulties.

References

California Department of Education (CDE). (2001). *California physical fitness test: Report to the governor and legislature.* Sacramento, CA: California Department of Education Standards and Assessment Division.

Castelli, D. M., Hillman, C. H., Buck, S. M., & Erwin, H. E. (2007). Physical fitness and academic achievement in third-and fifth-grade students. *Journal of Sport and Exercise Psychology, 29*(2), 239.

Dwyer, T., Sallis, J. F., Blizzard, L., Lazarus, R., & Dean, K. (2001). Relation of academic performance to physical activity and fitness in children. *Pediatric Exercise Science, 13*(3), 225-237.

Gardner, K. (2012, October 10). When Is The Best Time To Exercise? *The Gleaner*. Retrieved from http://jamaica-gleaner.com/gleaner/20121010/news/news2.html

Grissom, J. A (2005). Study of the Relationship Between Physical Fitness and Academic Achievement in California Using 2004 Test Results.

Hillman, C. H., Castelli, D. M., & Buck, S. M. (2005). Aerobic fitness and neurocognitive function in healthy preadolescent children. *Medicine and Science in Sports and Exercise, 37*(11), 1967.

Linder, K. J. (1999). Sport Participation and Perceived Academic Performance of School Children and Youth. *Pediatric Exercise Science,* 11, 129-144.

Mitchell, D. L. (1994, May). *The relationship between rhythmic competency and academic performance in first grade children.* Doctoral Dissertation. Orlando, FL: University of Central Florida Department of Exceptional and Physical Education.

Physical Exercise For Brain Health (2012). Retrieved from *Posit Science* at http://www.positscience.com/brain-resources/everyday-brain-fitness/physical-exercise

Safe Route To Schools (n.d.) *The Relationship Between Physical Activity, Weight, and Academic Achievement.* Retrieved from http://www.saferoutespartnership.org

Christy, S., & Martin, G. S. Physical and Psychological Predictors of Academic Performance For Middle School Boys and Girls: A Longitudinal Investigation.

Santos, F. (2011, October 19). Fitting In Exercise, Between Math and English *The New York Times.* Retrieved from http://www.nytimes.com

Taras H. (2005). Physical activity and student performance at school. *Journal of Scholastic Health,* 75(6), 214-218.

University of Illinois at Urbana-Champaign (2009, April 1). Physical Activity May Strengthen Children's Ability To Pay Attention.

Vail, K. (2006). Mind and body. *American School Board Journal,* 193(3), 30.

Vanaman, B. (2011, March 4). *How Exercise Affects the Brain.* Livestrong.com. Retrieved from http://www.livestrong.com/article/397005-how-exercise-affects-the-brain/

Chapter 12: The Law of Readiness

By failing to prepare, you are preparing to fail

—Benjamin Franklin

Colors fade, temples crumble, empires fall, but wise words endure

—Edward Thorndike

The Laws of Learning

Edward Lee Thorndike was a first among equals in the field of modern education psychology. Known as the father of modern educational psychology, Thorndike wrote the book on modern comparative psychology and dedicated his life to the study of human learning, education, and mental testing. His original interests included trying to understand learning in animals before he transitioned to studying learning in human beings.

His doctoral study of how animals learned disabused the standing presumption of animals' use of extraordinary faculties to gain critical insight in the solutions of the problems they faced. As he would recount, "In the first place, most of the books do not give us a psychology, but rather a eulogy of animals. They have all been about animal intelligence, never about animal stupidity" (Thorndike, 1911). His experiments showed that animal learning followed an *S*-curve or gradual learning curve, where rapid improvements are eventually replaced with a plateau effect.

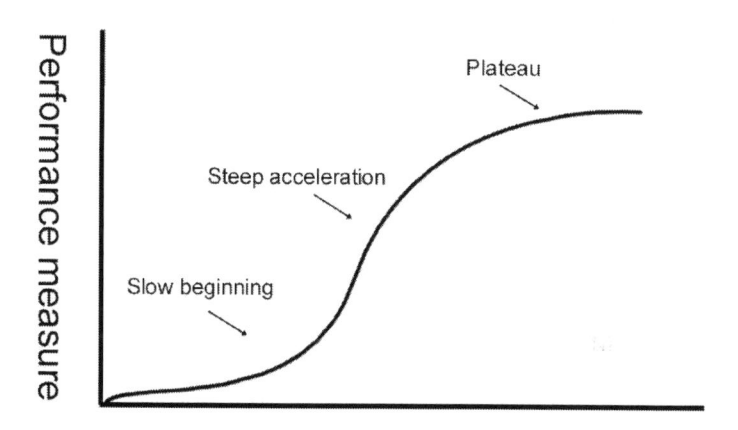

Number of trials or attempts at learning [15]

Thorndike elaborated a theory of learning—and this book is directly indebted to the contributions he made through experimental observations of the processes by which learning is encouraged or discouraged. His theory identifies three major laws, including the law titled in this chapter—the law of readiness. Thorndike noted that when it came to learning there were two states a person could occupy: a state of readiness or unreadiness.

Readiness to learn

The question is then: what makes a person ready to learn? Alternatively, to borrow the phrase from Malcolm Gladwell—what is the learning "tipping point" (Gladwell, 2000)? The following proverb, of unknown eastern or middle-eastern progeny is apropos to this interrogation:

He who knows not and knows not he knows not:
he is a fool—shun him.

He who knows not and knows he knows not:
he is simple—teach him.

He who knows and knows not he knows:
he is asleep—wake him.

He who knows and knows he knows:
he is wise—follow him.

The above suggests, among multiple things, that it is when we recognize our own ignorance that we are in a position to begin a movement to knowledge or enlightenment. This realization does not result in immediate illumination, but is an ingredient in tipping us over the point that separates unreadiness from readiness. It is, effectively, a turning point that leads to a tipping point.

Several other factors contribute to our willingness to "tip-over". These include the following. The first factor is the degree to which we perceive that the object of learning is "easy" or "achievable". The second factor is our belief in our ability to learn, which may be skewed toward the verdict proffered by the most recent history of past successes or failures in learning, and in learning something new (Thorndike's second and third laws). The final factor is our ability to persevere in the face of an "annoying state of affairs"—which would discourage further learning.

Critically, this book argues that when we are psychologically, emotionally, physically, and socially ready, then learning is not only accessible and satisfying, but can be accomplished with powerful results. To paraphrase Thorndike, the proverb from above would be rendered as follows:

If not ready, not learning is satisfying;

If ready, not learning is annoying;

If not ready, learning is annoying;

If ready, learning is satisfying (Gerber, 1999).

The goal of the learner then is unequivocally plain: to be ready to learn and by way of a corollary, to stay ready to learn.

Getting prepared

Effective preparation, therefore, triangulates the following: first, a belief that the task or goal one is pursuing is interesting or important; second, a belief that one can be successful at achieving the task (i.e., a sense of self-efficacy); and finally, a willingness to persevere even in the face of initial disappointments and setbacks. The following strategies provide actionable recommendations to improve organization for learning, because "students need to have both the 'will' and the 'skill' to be successful in classrooms" (Pintrich, et al., 1990). To this end, we provide notes on the following items, which research indicates are important determinants of success in the classroom.

Time Management

Being organized is a skill that appreciates three things: the nature of the tasks that must be accomplished; how long they will take; and, the resources that will be required to complete those tasks. This is the task-time-tools approach to self-organization. Research shows that on-campus involvement tends not to have any effect on time put into academic work outside of the classroom, i.e., students make it work (Hlavac, Peterson, & Piscioneri, 2011). However, by reducing the time one spends on passive leisure activities—playing computer/video games, hanging out with friends, watching television/movies—one can positively improve academic outcomes (Brint &

Cantwell, 2008; George et al., 2008). Contrarily, spending time with family encouraged academic achievement (Brint & Cantwell, 2008) while spending more time working at a job tended to lower academic achievement (Brint & Cantwell, 2008; McCormick, 2001; Plant et al., 2005).

Table 1. Time Management Strategies [16]

Tasks	Time	Tools
Set goals and priorities. Do first things first. There is always enough time for the important things.	Estimate your time realistically. Pay attention to how much work you can do in a certain period of time, and how quickly you actually read that Physics chapter. Be sure and set deadlines for yourself whenever possible.	Create and revise a study schedule accounting for the 168 hours in a week. Include classes, homework, eating, sleeping, exercise, sleeping, socializing, sleeping, clubs, down time.
Consider school your job. Expect to do a minimum of 1 hour of homework per lecture hour and 2 hours of study per lecture hour	Do your school work/job before your relaxation. Concentrate on one thing at a time. Reward yourself after a good day of studying	Make up a "To Do" list based on your priorities. The to-do list may be daily; weekly; bi-weekly; monthly; and quarterly.
Prioritize: Not all assignments are equal, and some courses will be more important or more difficult for you.	Seek balance. Do something new. Redeem the time and make every attempt to get satisfaction out of every moment.	Keep track of what you accomplish each day, and compare it to your short-term, medium term, and long-term priorities and goals.

Tasks	Time	Tools
Reduce distractions. Work away from your room, and TURN OFF your technology.	When you catch yourself procrastinating-ask yourself, "What am I avoiding?" Delegate responsibilities whenever possible. Practice just doing it.	Try to use waiting time-- review notes or do practice problems Put up reminders in your home or office about your goals

An important aspect of time management, as it relates to the daily life of the student, is getting the right routines in place before the start of classes each day. The following table organizes some important strategies and recommendations.

Table 2. Organization Strategies Before Class Starts

Planning	Scheduling:	Administering	Keeping committed
Keep a planner to keep track of assignments, tasks, projects, quizzes, tests	use term planners; weekly and daily planners; study plans or study timetables	Organize your study space/ desk area;	Find peer support-use a friend to help you stay on track.
Periodically review planner/ diary for upcoming deadlines	Get to classes at least five minutes before they start Sit near to the front of the class	Put your notes in binders with tabs, file folders or note pads; Download notes from the Web before each class.	Find someone who is very organized as your role model.
Have a things to do and things done tray/ folder	Bring a loose-leaf notebook; prepare pages ahead of time using the Cornell Method.	Find old exams early in the term.	Find someone you can go to the library with every day.
Keep papers in chronological order.	Long Term Schedule Construct a schedule of your fixed commitments only for each month.	At the beginning of the term review your course outline or syllabus to note the value or weighting of each assignment. Write the assignment AND its weighting on your term calendar.	Make a contract to get organized. List what you will do. Review it regularly.
Organize resources and materials the night before	Make a short list of MAJOR EVENTS and AMOUNT OF WORK to be accomplished in each subject this week. This may include non-study activities.	Analyze the course: Will tests tend to be objective? Is there outside reading? What are the assignments & grading policies? Look for exam topics during lectures.	Use technology such as software scheduling programs.

Planning	Scheduling:	Administering	Keeping committed
Have a designated place for your materials and resources	Each evening or early in the morning make out a specific daily schedule. Write down specifically what is to be done and cross out as you go.	Study section by section. Use lecture to clarify and review Otherwise, survey the chapter, skim, and ask yourself questions you would like to have answered during the lecture.	

Skills for Learning: During the Class

To grow as a student one must be committed to the process of improving one's study habits and study skills. Prior to this, it is important to develop those traits that will be helpful in deepening engagement with the content, and in improving ability to relate to more complex ways of being tested on the course materials. Foundational skills include good note taking, the ability to take tests well, memorization, listening, and problem solving. These are critical skills, which contribute to academic success (Rozalski, 2008).

Table 3. Note-taking and Listening for Learning

Writing	Coping/ Resources	Listening and Asking
Take notes: this can aid in the retention of lecture materials; Adequate notes are a necessary adjunct to efficient study and learning in college.	Bring pens, notebook, and textbook. Take and keep notes in a large notebook.	Remain open-minded to instructor/ lecture style: Deductive Inductive Topical Random.
Use the Cornell Method Label and date each page. Write legibly and on one side of your paper only It is better to err on the side of writing too much than too little; Try to listen, think, and note the major points; Sometimes it may be necessary to write first and think later	After a confusing lecture, refer back to your text or see your instructor

Be open minded about points you disagree on. Don't let arguing interfere with your note-taking. | Listen actively - if possible think before you write - but don't get behind

Focus on the major points.
Be alert to cues about what the professor thinks is important. |

Writing	Coping/ Resources	Listening and Asking
Highlight key phrases, concepts, meanings, formulas Put main ideas in margin: indent details Circle unfamiliar words; mark confusing ideas. Make your own short-hand	Accept that you may not be able to understand everything as it is introduced; Therefore, look over your notes as soon as possible	Listen for cues as to important points, transition, repetition, inflection, enumeration of a series of points.
Review notes regularly Summarize in your own words		Participate in discussions.
Leave a few spaces blank as you move from one point to the next so that you can fill in additional points later.		Ask questions if you don't understand
Copy down everything on the board		Ask for explanation if work is unclear

It is important to recognize that learning, practising, and mastering these skills occur in stages. They require intentional effort initially, but after extended period of practising time, the student can engage these tasks without undue reflection. The process of learning to drive and mastering the skill of driving is an immediate analogy that can be drawn. This model of skill acquisition is richly elaborated by American philosopher Professor Hubert Dreyfus:

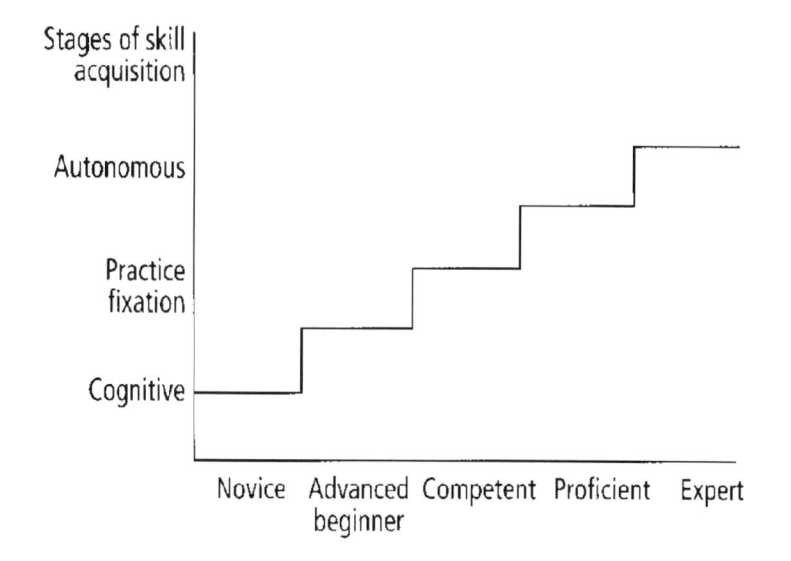

```
Stages of skill
   acquisition


Autonomous                              ┌─────────
                                        │
                            ┌───────────┘
Practice                    │
fixation        ┌───────────┘
                │
Cognitive ──────┘

              Novice  Advanced  Competent  Proficient  Expert
                      beginner
```

Source: Ericsson, K. A. (2011). Can We Create Gifted People by Deliberate Practice?

Acquiring a new skill takes time and is a process that goes through stages that witness increased competence. The more we practise, and especially critically review the cognitive and skills gaps in order to focus on targeted improvement, the better the level of expertise and mastery.

Revision: Learning and Relearning

To secure newly taught materials, it is important to revisit it frequently and early. Questions arising out of the lecture, and confusing or unclear points raised, should be resolved. At this stage, post-lecture, the seed must be watered and watched so that the full fruit of understanding may be harvested.

Table 4. Maximizing Learning after Lecture

Revision	Follow-up
Go back over notes within 24 hours; main ideas, key terms, and leading questions should be written in the margins.	Review often: Look at the preceding lecture notes carefully before class.
Label/date each page. Underline essentials in red, fill-in gaps. Write headings/key words/ questions in margins.	Look over notes before beginning any new study session. Question yourself about concepts/vocabulary. Map certain sections. Recopy your notes if necessary.
Write a brief summary. Relate lecture notes to text, look for overlap, transfer from text to lecture notes.	In the next lecture, ask questions raised from previous lecture; or from notes on lecture

Deliberate Practice

Part of this processing of learning and relearning is to guide a "deliberate practice" approach, which says that it is not about the quantity of time spent studying or learning material: it is the quality of time. Quality time means understanding where the cognitive gaps or weaknesses are, and seeking to fill those gaps. That is why reflection and evaluation after class, after homework, or after a variety of assessment exercises, is always a good expenditure of time. The following table identifies some key questions that we should answer post-test, or post-quiz, or post-homework.

Table 5. Analyzing Performance on an Assessment Exercises

Test/Quiz Analysis: Quick Analysis (Yes/No)	Extended analysis
Did you feel well-prepared?	Did you miss a lot of answers from any one particular chapter? If so, why? (Didn't study it; didn't understand the material; notes were inadequate, etc
Did you "cram" the night before?	Where did you miss most of your points?
Did your mind "go blank" at any time?	Which test questions did you answer correctly by guessing?
Did you have time to check your answers?	Which test questions didn't you expect, and why?
Was the book emphasized more than you expected it to be? Were you surprised by your grade?	What can you do to improve your next test score? (Study/review continually; seek a tutor; ask more questions; meet with your professor, etc.)

APPENDIX

THE CORNELL SYSTEM [17]

The Cornell system for taking notes is designed to save time but yet be highly efficient. There is no rewriting or retyping of your notes. It is a "DO IT RIGHT IN THE FIRST PLACE" system.

1. First Step—PREPARATION

Use a large, loose-leaf notebook. Use only one side of the paper. (You then can lay your notes out to see the direction of a lecture.) Draw a vertical line 2 1/2 inches from the left side of your paper. This is the recall column. Notes will be taken to the right of this margin. Later key words or phrases can be written in the recall column.

2. Second Step—DURING THE LECTURE

Record notes in paragraph form. Capture general ideas, not illustrative ideas. Skip lines to show end of ideas or thoughts. Using abbreviations will save time. Write legibly.

3. Third Step—AFTER THE LECTURE

Read through your notes and make it more legible if necessary. Now use the column. Jot down ideas or key words, which give you the idea of the lecture. (REDUCE) You will have to reread the lecturer's ideas and reflect in your own words. Cover up the right-hand portion of your notes and recite the general ideas and concepts of the lecture. Overlap your notes showing only recall columns and you have your review.

References

Brint, S., Cantwell, A. M., & Hanneman, R. A. (2008). The two cultures of undergraduate academic engagement. *Research in Higher Education, 49*(5), 383-402.

Gerber, S. (1999). Enhancing Counselor Intervention Strategies: An Integrational Viewpont. Taylor & Francis.

George, D., Dixon, S., Stansal, E., Gelb, S. L., & Pheri, T. (2008). Time diary and questionnaire assessment of factors associated with academic and personal success among college undergraduates. *Journal of American College Health, 56*(6), 706-715.

Gladwell, M. (2000). The tipping point: How little things can make a big difference. Little, Brown.

Hlavac, J., Peterson, J., & Piscioneri, M. (2011). Time allocations for study: Evidence from Arts students in Australia. *Education+ Training, 53*(1), 27-44.

McCormick, A. C. (2001). It's about time: what to make of reported declines. *Liberal Education, 97*(1), 30-39.

Pintrich, P. R., & De Groot, E. V. (1990). Motivational and self-regulated learning components of classroom academic performance. *Journal of educational psychology, 82*(1), 33.

Plant, A. E., Ericsson, K. A., Hill, L., & Asberg, A. (2005). Why study time does not predict grade point average across college students: implications of deliberate practice for academic performance. *Contemporary Educational Psychology, 30*, 96-116.

Rozalski, M. E. (2008). Practice, practice, practice: how to improve student's study skills. *Beyond Behavior*, *17*(2), 17-23.
Thorndike, Edward (1911). *Animal Intelligence*. Macmillan. p. 22

Thorndike, E. L. (1911). Animal Intelligence, 2nd ed. New York, NY: Hafner. Transaction Publishers, 2000.

CHAPTER 13: THE LAW OF STUDY AND DELIBERATE PRACTICE

A mind of moderate capacity which closely pursues one study must infallibly arrive at great proficiency in that study.

— Mary Shelley, Frankenstein

Exploring self-regulated learning

Educational researchers have recently begun to identify and study key processes through which students take ownership of their academic learning. This process of ownership is called self-regulation. Previously, studies have not focused on the learner, but on strategies of lesson delivery, methods used by teachers, and what can be done externally to help students. It is, however, of equal importance that students exert effort by studying what they have been exposed. In the past, there has been little research on the empirical evidence about how students become masters at self-regulated learning.

According to self-regulated learning guru, Barry Zimmerman (2002), "the attainment of optimal academic performance requires more than high quality instruction and requisite mental ability on the part of the students: it requires personal initiative, diligence, and self-directive skill." He further confirms that the use of these skills has a substantial correlation with academic achievement. He gives us a working definition of self-regulation as "self-generated thoughts, feelings, and actions that are planned and cyclically adapted to the attainment of personal goals" (Zimmerman, 2002). In other words, self-regulated learning is the process of taking control of, and evaluating, one's learning and learning behavior (Ormrod, 2009).

The DNA of the self-regulated learner

Fourteen traits characterize the self-regulated learner. These are captured in the table below. As Zimmerman reiterates in another research article, "Students' use of these self-regulated learning strategies was strongly associated with superior academic functioning" (Zimmerman, 1990).

Table 6. Cognitive Strategies Of Self-Regulated Learner

Categories of Strategies	Definitions
Self-evaluation	Student-initiated evaluations of the quality or progress of their work
Organizing and transforming information	Rearrangement of instructional materials
Goal-setting and planning	Setting of goals and subgoals and planning of sequencing, timing, and completing activities related to goals.
Seeking information	Efforts to secure further tasks information from nonsocial sources
Keeping records and monitoring	Efforts to record events or results
Environmental structuring	Selecting or arranging the physical setting to make learning easier
Self-consequences	Arrangement of rewards or punishments for success or failure.
Rehearsing and memorizing	Efforts to memorize material by through practice.
Seeking social assistance	Solicitation of help from peers, teachers, and adults
Reviewing records	Rereading of test, notes, or textbooks to prepare for class or future test.
Other	Learning behavior that is initiated by others such as teachers or parents.

Many activities and strategies can be employed by self-regulated students to improve academic outcomes. The key element of self-regulated learning, of course, is the student. All other factors surround the student, and success depends on the effectiveness of the strategies employed by the student. There are four sub-areas involved in self-regulated learning: planning, monitoring, regulation, and social contact.

This chapter addresses how the traits of self-regulation are applied to effective studying. It recognizes that effective students set goals that are important and interesting to them. This keeps them motivated to learning and mastering the material they are studying, as well as motivated to developing their skills as a learner while managing their efforts at learning (Paris, Lipson & Wixson, 1983; Pintrich, 1988, 1989; Pintrich, Cross, Kozma, & McKeachie, 1986).

Self-regulated learners monitor how well they are doing in achieving their goals, and are emotionally resilient, therefore persevering even when the task at hand is challenging, blocking out distractions like noisy classmates, maintaining their focus on the task, and enabling superior academic achievement (Corno, 1986; Corno & Rohr Kemper, 1985; Fincham & Cain; 1986; Paris & Oka, 1986; Schunk, 1985).

Capable students think about how they can learn, retain, and comprehend the material employing such strategies as doing their own research, clarifying the materials with peers or the teacher, rehearsing lecture notes, elaborating or extending lecture notes, and organizing or rearranging their lecture notes to show greater connectivity and development of core ideas. In other words, capable students not only *know* the strategies for effective learning and studying, they are motivated to *use* them, and to *keep using* them. Some of these strategies are developed below.

Help seeking, Peer Learning, and Social Control

The independent learner proactively seeks information when needed, and takes the necessary steps to understand and to master this information. The process of comprehending the taught material may mean accessing suitable recommended readings or doing additional research on the topics. This means understanding how to use a library, becoming proficient with Internet search engines, reviewing notecards, and ensuring that notes, texts, and tests are reread.

The student should also seek assistance when necessary from peers, teachers, and knowledgeable others. When I was doing my Master's in financial mathematics, and found myself on the wrong end of the stochastic calculus stick— and if you don't know what stochastic calculus is, you understand precisely how I felt—I surveyed the Internet for similar courses, and found professors who lectured in the field. I would send untold numbers of emails requesting help, especially when stuck with an assignment. Sometimes, I even emailed the authors of the text! Of course, if you are not comfortable with sometimes being rejected, I do not recommend this sort of email adventure!

Bennett (2011) found the social aspect of learning to be important in contributing to academic performance. He highlighted the critical roles of: discussing classroom materials with peers outside of lessons; discussing lecture materials with the teacher outside of class; collaborative studying when necessary; interacting with persons from different ethnic background and with different values; and, setting aside time for independent or personal studies. Research supports the claim that our peers do have an effect on our academic performance—and having a roommate, who loves gaming for example, can reduce our academic performance. As Stinebrickner and Stinebrickner (2007) find, "video games can have a large causal effect on academic outcomes."

Organizing and Transforming Information

This means that students identify the important aspects that need to be studied, thus eliminating unnecessary information. This approach involves students outlining required or important information, which can then be further highlighted. This can be done at the time of learning. From there the students can make summaries, which, if done correctly, can demonstrate their understanding of the concept.

Once a student understands a concept, then that student is able to rearrange the material in such a way that integrates and connects the information, thus allowing the student to go beyond just listing or naming to being able to justify based on understanding of underlying concepts. At this point, the student is then able to make flash cards or index cards, and even depict such information on charts, diagrams, pictures, or with the use of webs or mappings.

Rehearsing and Memorizing

There are a number of strategies available to help us to remember. These include: use of mnemonic devices; teaching someone else the material; making sample questions; using repetition; and visualization (drawing mental pictures). These are explained and tabled below.

Mnemonic Devices	Teaching someone else the material	Making sample questions
1. Music 2. Name 3. Expression or word 4. Model 5. Ode or Rhyme 6. Note organization 7. Image 8. Connection 9. Spelling	Students enlisted to tutor others, work harder to understand the material. Consequently, they recall it more accurately, and apply it more effectively. In what scientists label as "the protégé effect," student teachers score higher on tests than pupils who are learning for their own sake.	This gets the mind in the frame of answering such questions. It anticipates possible quiz or examination questions and provides the opportunity to engage in study and self-testing, which improves retention. It also makes studying an active rather than passive process.

Figure 13.1 Rehearsing and memorizing strategies

Using mental imagery	Using repetition
Mental imagery involves the student imagining herself performing a specific activity while using all her senses. It is a skill that can be used to reach specific goals. This causes more realistic self-expectation and thus makes it easier to stick to the study regime.	Repetition is used to give emphasis to particular word, phrase or idea. Whatever is being repeated is what the person wants to remember.

Figure 13.2 Rehearsing and memorizing strategies

Environment management

The environment in which one studies can enhance a student's attitude, reception, or retention of information. A student is able to identify the environment in which she is comfortable. Therefore, it is up to the student to select, structure, and create environments that optimize learning, by enabling sustained focus and deeper-level understanding. She should also consider how environment affects learning, seeking out places that are most likely to encourage application; places that are quiet and with limited distractions. One of my favorite study haunts while as a graduate student at Florida State University in

Tallahassee was the local Burger King: it was close, relatively quiet, and had the convenience of large desk spaces, food, and a restroom nearby!

Unsurprisingly, studying and engaging in social activities, like Facebook, or talking in person to friends while studying, tends to diminish the effectiveness of the learning time (Winter et al, 2010). Having a distraction-free environment encourages improved academic performance throughout the semester and throughout college in general (Plant et al., 2005). Additionally, how a student views her learning environment can have more substantial effect than her academic ability. If the learning environment is perceived to be more about partying, drinking, and "having a good time," then socializing will overtake studying as the premier focus of one's free time. Rau and Durand (2000) unsurprisingly found that learning environments that attract high-level drinking are not effective learning environments as heavy drinking disrupts the academic life of the drinker, as well as that of other students within close proximity.

The student must learn to structure her learning environment to meet her particular study needs. It has to be noted that no one method or environment works for everyone. Therefore, the student has to be able to assess herself and know what is suitable for her particular situation. This includes selecting and arranging the physical setting: some people work better with a desk and a chair, some might be more comfortable on the floor, on a cushion, or on a comforter.

It is best to eliminate or minimize distractions, therefore studying in an area that is isolated from the noise of television, radio, or even from other people is recommended. One has to be smart, use moderation, and ensure that study periods are broken up and spread over time. Studying in different places, and studying different topics, helps by putting less strain on the eyes, and limits the chances of getting bored.

External factors affecting self-regulated learning

Another factor that can affect studying is incorrect or misinterpreted information. This can result from a misunderstanding of texts, or not copying notes correctly from the book or board. However, it could involve external factors such as poor study conditions, confusing teachers, hard-to-understand textbooks, or the illegibility of writings on the board. The student therefore has to ensure that these factors are eliminated by seeking clarification, cross-checking information, and having a clear idea as to what situations work best for her. This understanding comes with practice and experimenting with various study conditions.

Self-regulated learning strategies

- **Organize and transform information**: this means making the information work for you by representing it diagrammatically, and using tables or charts in order to see development and connection of ideas.

- **Rehearse and memorize**: This can come from studying and re-writing relevant formulas, or problem solving where the relevant methods, techniques, or ideas are rehearsed and constantly used. Consequently, rehearsing information can be in the context of problem solving, or as a stand-alone process, verbally reciting from note-cards. In addition, this includes reviewing notes, books, or tests in order to learn/master the content.
- **Apply learning:** many subjects go beyond the usual reading and require practice. Therefore, in her study time, the student has to go through exercises such as end-of-unit/chapter testing. She can also seek supplemental texts for additional exercises.
- **Do the work:** the student has to ensure that the work is done. She has to complete assignments, engage in practical coursework or projects, and avoid the

temptation to procrastinate. It means work first, and play second.

- **Alternate study environment:** By studying in one area for too long, the student might miss the essence of what is to be studied, leading to diminishing returns on study time. Additionally, research shows that studying in different places improves retention. As Benedict Carey (2010) elegantly puts it, "Forcing the brain to make multiple associations with the same material may, in effect, give that information more neural scaffolding."

- **Mix study topics:** Studying distinct but related topics can strengthen understanding by deepening the connections between the concepts. Someone learning a new language might mix vocabulary, with reading, and speaking. An athlete might work on strength, speed, and skill in one session.

- **Study consistently:** having a study timetable breaks

down the workload of the brain, and reduces the need for panic-driven cramming. By gradually and regularly saturating the mind with the course content—reviewing the material daily, weekly, monthly—neural connections are strengthened, and retention is improved, even beyond the life of the course.

- **Do practice tests, quizzes, essays:** for some, learning is fundamentally about recall and self-testing is a powerful tool toward this end. Doing practice assessment activities encourages the brain to recall the stored memory, and the effort of this process changes and strengthens the memory of the thing recalled, making future recall easier. As Dr. Henry Roedigger III, psychologist at Washington University states, "Testing not only measures knowledge but changes it" and changes it by giving it a greater ease in recall (Carey, 2010). Research indicates that the study session-then-testing session routine may be better than having a train of study sessions with a testing session tacked on at the end (Carey, 2010). Additionally, having a mix of difficulty level of questions practised during self-testing is good as the "harder it is to remember something, the harder it is to later forget" (Carey, 2010).

- **Select, structure, and create environments to optimize learning:** As was discussed earlier, the environment plays a vital role in giving the students the ability to focus well. Eliminating distractions and varying study locations adds efficiency and effectiveness to study routines.

- **Seek help:** Seek out information by asking others such as peers, teachers, authority figures who might be able to shed some light and thus provide additional information, or even clarification.

- **Do your own research:** the text or handout may not provide important details for a given topic; or, the information may be abstruse or unclear. Therefore, clarification can be sought from other sources.

Study and Learning Strategies [18]

The four major study and learning strategies are: note taking, active study, organization, and forming study groups. Before actually engaging in study, one has to take notes, whether given by the teacher or from textbooks. Proper note taking is essential as this eliminates incorrect information being retained in memory. There are various areas that are involved in proper note taking. As an effective note-taker you should:

- Write neatly;
- Highlight key phrases;
- Review notes periodically;
- Summarize in your own words;
- Paraphrase the text/teacher;
- Invent a personal shorthand; and,
- Use titles, headings, and dates.

Then there is active study. There are three areas involved in active study. First, one should recite information. This involves repeating aloud what one is studying. This helps in rehearsing and memorizing notes. Second, write down what is being studied. This improves retention, personal organization, and facilitates revision. Finally, draw diagrams, charts, and use pictures as it helps in visualizing the answer. To paraphrase an important saying: Seeing is remembering!

The third study and learning strategy is organization. Organization can be both digital and physical. In this dimension you need to determine a system for storing information and retrieving information. The use of folders, trays, and binders are helpful in this area. Having a diary also helps to plan and provide reminders. Phones can provide tremendous support in helping one to organize reminders and store/access information when required.

Table 7. Activities to achieve proper organization.

Organization
• Have a timetable for homework, quizzes, projects, and exams
• Keep a to do/done folder
• Keep a reminder checklist
• Order materials chronologically
• Clean and reorganize regularly
• Pack book bag and gather materials prior to going to bed
• Have a set place for placing materials at home

Finally, in courses where the content is large and oftentimes inaccessible, having a study group can reduce the workload of breaking down the content and coming to deeper understanding by distributing the workload for greater learning effect. This has to be carefully done, as member selection is important so that no one is burdened while others are lightened.

Table 8. Study strategies: Forming a study group

Form a study group	Be productive with your time
work with 2-4 classmates or friends	Use "found-time": these are small amounts of time between classes or appointments. Use this time to help to get prepared for group meetings
rotate leadership	set a regular meeting time and place
keep all members informed of meetings and agenda	socialize for the first 10 minutes and perhaps last 10-15 minutes as part of the structure of the group, to avoid distractions during the work session
define objectives of the group: discuss homework questions, "teach" other members how to solve a problem, design potential exam questions and share answers	
if members are behind on readings, consider assigning 1 reading per member, and then each shares her summary of the reading	

Conclusion

There are many stories, precepts, and routines that have been marshaled to assisting the learner in understanding those factors which contribute to efficient and effective learning. We must start from inside: believe right, persevere, stay motivated. We must also manage right: have the right goals, condition our bodies to maintain and sustain our journey, and have a physical and social environment that encourages goal accomplishment. Finally, we complete the palette of observations with effective study routines to internalize the things taught, and make them a part of our own neural networks.

Genius, and the success it attracts, is dynamic and inventive. It holds a curiosity about the world that is undaunted by failure: rather seeing failure as part of the journey to success. If we would achieve the promise of our intellectual potential we must be willing to experiment, to practise, to persevere, and to think about our learning in an extended way that shows that we realize how important an investment it is we are making in our lives. For to learn is to own the future, our future.

References

Bennett, S. (2011). Learning behaviors and learning spaces. *Libraries and the Academy, 11*(3), 765-789.

Carey, B. (2010, September 6). Forget What You Know About Good Study Habits. *The New York Times.* Retrieved from http://www.nytimes.com/

Corno, L. (1986). The metacognitive control components of self-regulated learning. *Contemporary Educational Psychology, 11*(4), 333-346.

Corno, L., & Rohrkemper, M. (1985). The intrinsic motivation to learn in classrooms. *Research on motivation in education, 2*, 53-90.

Fincham, F. D., & Cain, K. M. (1986). Learned helplessness in humans: A developmental analysis. *Developmental Review, 6*(4), 301-333.

Kivinen, K. (2010) *Motivation and Self-Regulated Learning—From Theory To Practice.* Retrieved from http://kivinen.files.wordpress.com/2012/04/motivation-and-srl.pdf

Ormrod, Jeanne Ellis (2009). *Essentials of educational psychology*, 2nd edition. Upper Saddle River, New Jersey: Pearson.

Paris, S. G., & Oka, E. R. (1986). Children's reading strategies, metacognition, and motivation. *Developmental Review, 6*(1), 25-56.

Paris, S. G., Lipson, M. Y., & Wixson, K. K. (1983). Becoming a strategic reader. *Contemporary educational psychology, 8*(3), 293-316.

Pintrich, P. R. (1988). A process-oriented view of student motivation and cognition. *New directions for institutional research*, (57), 65-79.

Pintrich, P. R. (1989). The dynamic interplay of student motivation and cognition in the college classroom. *Advances in motivation and achievement, 6*, 117-160.

Pintrich, P. R., Cross, D. R., Kozma, R. B., & McKeachie, W. J. (1986). Instructional psychology. *Annual Review of Psychology, 37*(1), 611-651.

Plant, A. E., Ericsson, K. A., Hill, L., & Asberg, A. (2005). Why study time does not predict grade point average across college students: implications of deliberate practice for academic performance. *Contemporary Educational Psychology, 30*, 96-116.

Rau, W, & Durand, A. (2000). The academic ethic and college grades: does hard work help students to "make the grade"? *Sociology of Education, 73*(1), 19-38.

Schunk, D. H. (1985). Self? efficacy and classroom learning. *Psychology in the Schools, 22*(2), 208-223.

Stinebrickner, R., & Stinebrickner, T. R. (2005). How much does studying matter? *Federal Reserve Bank of Cleveland Proceedings*, 55-59.

Winter, J., Cotton, D., Gavin, J., & Yorke, J. D. (2010). Effective e-learning? Multi-tasking, distractions and boundary management by graduate students in an online environment. *Association for Learning Technology Journal, 18*(1), 71-83.

Zimmerman, B. J. (1990). Self-regulated learning and academic achievement: An overview. *Educational psychologist, 25*(1), 3-17.

Zimmerman, B. J. (2002). Achieving academic excellence: A self-regulatory perspective. *The pursuit of excellence through education*, 85-110.

BIOGRAPHY OF THE AUTHOR

Palmer comes to this project of writing about the keys to genius with the credentials of one who has worked tirelessly to cultivate his love of learning. A voracious reader from a young age, he was champion speller at his primary school. Chess team captain, knowledge bowl captain, student council president—he blossomed during his high school career to finish amongst the top three students. On his way to student governance, he developed an undying love affair with words and essay writing.

A truly cosmopolitan intellectual, he has won national and international scholarships, studying at a top liberal arts college in the USA—Macalester College—renowned for its liberalism and intellectual rigor. Graduating just shy of a triple major, over the course of the next thirteen years he would complement this first degree with three master's degrees: Economics; Mathematical Sciences; and, Financial Mathematics. An international teacher and lecturer in mathematics, with instructional experience at the primary, secondary, and tertiary levels, Palmer presses into service his considerable experiences as an educator in the Caribbean, Europe, and the United States to unpack those keys intended to make learning "effortless doing."

[1] See McGuire, M (2010). Three Simple Words: A Rhetorical Analysis of the Slogan "Yes WE Can." *Advances in Communication Theory and Research, 3.* Retrieved from http://www.k-state.edu/actr/category/2010/default.htm

[2] First Battalion 50th Infantry Association (n.d.). *Vietnam Era War "Jargon."* Retrieved December 6, 2012 from http://www.ichiban1.org/html/history_glossary.htm#D

3] *Newton's First Law of Motion* (n.d.). Retrieved December 6, 2012 from http://www.physicsclassroom.com/class/newtlaws/u211a.cfm

[4] Moffit et al. (2011) would enlarge on this in their work, finding that self-control identified in the first 10 years of one's life predicted financial well-being, physical and psychological health, the lack of criminal convictions and drug use.

[5] By self-discipline we mean selecting the long-term gain over the short-term pleasure: keeping calm over throwing a temper tantrum; reading instructions before starting a test; paying attention in class rather than daydreaming; saving rather than spending; homework rather than television ("Self-Regulation Supports Student Learning and Achievement," 2009).

[6] Emotional Intelligence is the ability to interpret and control one's emotions, and that of other individuals and groups in order to promote emotional and intellectual growth (Mayer and Salovey, 1997). Daniel Goleman identifies five main domains of emotional intelligence: self-awareness; self-regulation (what I term self-discipline); social skill; empathy; and, motivation.

[7] See for further details, "Supersize Your Self-Control" at http://www.fitnessmagazine.com/weight-

loss/tips/diet-tips/tips-to-curb-cravings-strengthen-willpower/

[8] http://www.scientificamerican.com/article.cfm?id=-mind-reviews-the-honest-truth-about-dishonesty

[9] Adapted from the article titled Snooze or Lose (Bronson, 2007)

[10] Conscientiousness is one of the Big Five personality traits from Costa & McRae (1992), which sought to model relationship between personality and academic behaviors. The other traits include: Agreeableness (friendly vs. unkind), Neuroticism (nervous vs. confident), Openness (inventive vs. cautious), and Extraversion (outgoing vs. solitary). They can be remembered using the word mnemonic: CANOE. Conscientiousness refers to the measure of how efficient or organized one is—and at the extreme these are perfectionists and workaholics.

[11] Sardanapalus was a king of Assyria. He is supposed to have lived in the 7th century BC, and dies in an "orgy of destruction" after spending his life in decadent laziness, excess, and luxury. http://www.britannica.com/EBchecked/topic/524121/Sardanapalus; Sardanapalus. (2012-10-15).

[12] taken from http://www.archielsf.qc.ca/archie/moose.html description of the character from the comic

[13] A nationally recognized test that measures aerobic capacity, body composition, muscle strength, endurance, and flexibility

[14] America's most widely used admissions exam among colleges and universities

[15] http://www.intropsych.com/ch07_cognition/learning_curve.html

[16] http://www.dartmouth.edu/~acskills/success/time.html; and, http://www.queensu.ca/learningstrategies/undergrad/tm.html

[17] http://www.ucc.vt.edu/stdysk/cornell.html

[18] For further resources, see http://www.mbc.edu/academic/resources/study/memory.asp ; and http://www.ucc.vt.edu/stdysk/stdyhlp.html; and, http://www.studygs.net/

Printed in Great Britain
by Amazon.co.uk, Ltd.,
Marston Gate.